The Infinite Bond

Barbara Fox, DVM

The Infinite Bond

Barbara Fox, DVM

Front cover photograph and interior sketch from 123RF.com

All interior photos from Barbara Fox

Senior picture, p. 83, by Kohl1 Photography, Clermont, IA

Cover design & book layout by Laura Ashton
laura@gitflorida.com

ISBN: 978-1974002412

Printed in the United States of America

Dedication

To my three beautiful horses
~ Ibn, Ty, and Stormy ~
much gratitude for the companionship,
guidance, and wisdom you've shown me.
I love you for eternity.

Table of Contents

Foreword

This book was the most difficult writing assignment I've ever tackled. In one aspect, it is one of the most beautiful love stories between animals I've ever witnessed. On another, it was the most heart wrenching project, having to relive intimate details of my own life and the challenges of three of my best animal friends, dealing with the emotions that resurfaced after so many years. However, the lessons my "three boys" taught me have been invaluable, and I wish to share with you these incredible teachings.

As animal lovers, and people in general, are becoming acutely aware of the fact that animals have—and share—many of the same emotions that humans experience, it is my goal and mission to express what I have witnessed as a veterinarian for the past twenty-three years. Animals do grieve. Animals do express joy and happiness. Animals can be jealous, anxious, and fearful. Animals can be extremely entertaining. They can cause us to be impatient and demanding. They can be a great source of comfort to us when we are hurting. Animals can be a mirror into our own lives, giving us insight into what needs to be improved within us.

In my mind, and in my heart, I believe animals come to us in this earthly plane to be a companion, a guide, a teacher, and/or a protector, depending on our needs. Animals often find us. They will appear at the right place, the right time. All we need to do is be open to their attention and affection. How many times have you heard friends or acquaintances talk about the stray dog or cat that "just showed up?" There are no accidents, no coincidences in life. They appeared for a reason. And oftentimes we are totally unaware of why we were attracted to that particular animal.

Barbara Fox, DVM

None of our horses joined our family because of their blue ribbon show records, their great beauty, or their performance. Neither were the dogs or cats that joined our furry friend club. They were accepted to become part of our family because of their special needs, their affection, and their hearts. It saddens me to no end when an animal is rejected because of their lack of certain bloodlines, some imperfection in their structure, or because they're past their prime in the show ring. I remember well a saying in the movie Seabiscuit. This race horse suffered a potentially career-ending injury during his prime racing period. The recommendation was to put him down. "Tom," Seabiscuit's trainer, adamantly refused, saying, "You don't throw away a whole life just because just because he's banged up a little." Seabiscuit was given his chance to rally, and with careful rehabilitation and therapy, he went on to win one of the biggest events in race horse history. He also served to help his own jockey (Red) heal from a horrible injury when he was told he would never ride again.

The three Arabian geldings you will be introduced to changed my life in so many positive ways. Possessing so many different personalities, these boys were a great source of entertainment, comfort, education, and love. As you read the pages ahead, think of how your special animal companion(s) has touched your life and brought out the best in you. Immerse yourself in the relevance of your animal friend and be full of gratitude for his or her service on this earthly plane.

–Dr. Barb Fox

Chapter 1
Perceptions

The old, white horse stiffly walked across the front lawn, stopping every few steps to nibble a few blades of tender grass. He chewed slowly, savoring the rich flavor of the late spring vegetation. When he reached the northeast corner of the yard, the old boy halted. Standing squarely on all four feet, he stretched his thin neck forward and gazed out into the distant hayfields. For several minutes, he never moved except to blink. His soft brown eyes had a dreamy appearance, as though he was in another world.

Dahl Ibn Raghir had never been quieter in his twenty-one years of life. Effects from a chronic, debilitating medical condition had taken a major toll on his body. The gelding, who had been famous for entertaining his human admirers with a multitude of antics and tricks, was reduced to a crippled, frail creature due to complications from Cushing's syndrome. In his prime, Ibn (pronounced *Ibben*) could unseat an unsuspecting rider by inserting a well-placed buck at a full gallop. Usually, this occurred at an extremely inappropriate time, like at the state fair Rodeo Queen contest when my daughter, Carrie, was saluting the crowd. He was extremely intelligent, though this proved to be a curse many times, especially when it came to opening stall doors and gate latches. There was a time when Ibn cleverly lifted a chain from its notch on the gate, letting twenty-four horses out of the pasture. Fortunately, the horses stayed in the front yard of the stable owner's home instead of wandering down the gravel road.

I stared intently at Ibn, knowing in my heart that his time in this physical realm was limited. My husband, Gary, and I had recently had a heart-wrenching discussion about Ibn's future; we would not subject him to further suffering should he have another major setback in his health. At the present time, Ibn was eating well and his pain was being managed with conventional medications. However, I knew from dealing with many cases of the disease in veterinary practice that his condition could go south in a heartbeat. As if reading my mind, Ibn slowly turned his neck and looked directly at us.

I leaned forward over the wooden fence post and said sadly, "You know, Gary, Ibn doesn't have a lot of time left."

Gary looked down at the ground, cleared his throat, and replied, "I know. I sure don't want to see him suffer. He's been through enough." Ibn had been through a multitude of treatments, including surgery, corrective shoeing, acupuncture, and special diets. However, he continued to suffer frequent bouts of laminitis, a debilitating and painful foot condition associated with his metabolic disorder.

"The saddest thing," I continued, "is that I don't believe Ty will last much longer after Ibn passes." Tysheyn, our twenty-five year old Arabian, and Ibn had been inseparable buddies for the past twelve years. They wandered the pasture together, stopping in unison to check out an especially flavorful clump of grass, and napped side by side on the soft bed of pine shavings inside their shelter. They had been trailered to a multitude of horse shows and trail rides together over the past decade. Though at times the two geldings acted like two bickering little brothers, nipping incessantly at each other, they were best of friends. If one left sight of the other, there would be frantic whinnying until the other returned.

"You really think so? Ty letting go after Ibn's gone?" Gary questioned.

"It's just a feeling I have. They're *so* bonded." Tears welled up in my eyes at the thought of losing them.

Ty was grazing a few feet away from us. Except for a slight sway to his back and a few fuzzy gray hairs on his muzzle, Ty looked good for his age. His dark chestnut-colored haircoat and his exceptionally long, wispy mane glistened in the sunshine. Though Ty was officially "retired" from clinics and shows, I still enjoyed saddling him up for short rides around the farm.

"I sure hope you're wrong about your 'feeling,'" Gary responded.

"Me too, hon." I sighed and reached down to pick up the boys' lead ropes. Not wanting them to overindulge on the rich grass, we led them back to the pasture.

Stormy, our third Arabian gelding, trotted up to greet his pasture mates as I swung the corral gate open. The beautiful bay thirteen-year-old nickered as if to say, "Hey, why do *you* get all the attention?" There was some truth to that supposition, though, as Ibn's health issues had required a lot of time and dedication.

Little did anyone know that Stormy would receiving a *lot* more attention in the near future...

Chapter 2
Tysheyn

I pressed the phone tighter against my ear as I quickly scribbled notes concerning one of Lawrence Brown's horses. Lawrence hoped I could help decide whether his new Arabian show horse was "fixable" or if it needed to "go down the road." Lawrence had recently purchased Ty after learning that the horse had an impressive show record as a four-and five-year-old in English Pleasure. Ty was now six and his previous owners were anxious to sell. Lawrence thought he had gotten a "deal" since he purchased Ty for a fraction of what a really good English Pleasure show horse would bring. Now Lawrence was concerned he bought a lemon.

"So, Lawrence," I asked, "what did you say exactly was going on with Ty?" I knew from experience that issues between horse and rider were usually from poor communication between the two and not an unwillingness of the horse to cooperate. In my mind, it was imperative that the horse be given the benefit of the doubt.

"Like I explained, he doesn't want to turn to the right and if you put *any* kind of pressure on the right rein, he tries to rear up." Lawrence's voice rose in pitch as his frustration escalated. "I'm just about ready to send him to that big auction in Minnesota next weekend," he sighed. "I can't afford to get hurt at my age."

"So you said that the horse was always in the ribbons a year ago, right? What's he been doing since? Has he been shown or even ridden since then?" I quizzed.

"No idea," Lawrence offered. "I guess I assumed he was still being shown. Now I'm wondering why I haven't seen him on the show circuit."

"Well, why don't you bring him over to the stable tomorrow and at least let me try him out. I hate to see any horse go to an auction." I was moonlighting as a riding instructor and show trainer at a local boarding stable. "I'll hop on him and see if I can troubleshoot the problem."

"Okay, I guess you can give him a try. I'd sure like to see what you think," Lawrence replied. "See you around two o'clock."

The next afternoon, the tall, dark, chestnut gelding stepped off the trailer hesitantly, trembling as he surveyed his surroundings. Lawrence led him carefully through the sliding doors into the barn. The whites of Ty's eyes were visible as he took in the whirlwind of activity surrounding him. Stable hands pushed overflowing manure carts down the cement aisle, wheels squeaking and grinding under the weight of their contents. A handler exercising a young training horse in the indoor arena cracked a bullwhip, making Ty jump. A stallion toward the rear of the barn struck his feet against the stall door repeatedly, capturing Ty's focus and causing him to prance in place.

Since the stall where Ty would temporarily be housed wasn't yet clean, Lawrence turned his new horse out in the outdoor arena. As soon as he unsnapped the rope from Ty's halter, Ty bounded into a bold, animated trot. With his head held high in the air and his ultra-long mane and tail whipping in the breeze as he flaunted his lofty, ground-covering trot, Ty was the epitome of the perfect English Pleasure horse. If I could discover the cause for Ty's odd behavior under saddle, this horse would always be in the ribbons for the Browns.

After several minutes of continuous trotting and galloping, Ty stopped along the far side of the circular arena. His nostrils flared and sweat glistened on the gelding's chest. Concerned that he would become overheated in the hot sun, I decided to move him to small paddock that had big maple trees where he could get shade. Ty watched me warily. The whites of his eyes were visible, and the muscles along his spine and chest began quivering as I approached. I stopped momentarily and softly called to him, "Hey, buddy, it's alright. Whoa, boy." He remained still, unsure about the woman approaching his space. I stepped toward him, offering the back of my hand as a "greeting." Fear dominated, and Ty quickly spun around and galloped to an area farthest away from me, then stopped. I gave him a minute to settle, then tried the quiet approach again. Ty whirled and ran in the opposite direction. Lawrence also attempted to help corner the evasive gelding, but Ty wanted nothing to do with being caught.

Had it not been for the fear in his eyes and the apprehensive body language, I would have thought Ty was just being stubborn. But there was something deep and mysterious about the gelding's behavior that puzzled me. Exhausted from trying to capture him, I placed a few large flakes of hay and a bucket of fresh water in the arena and left Ty alone for the night.

It wasn't until late the next afternoon that I was able to slide a lead rope cautiously around Ty's neck. "Good boy," I praised, as Ty submissively lowered his head and pushed his nose into the leather halter. I stroked his neck and gently massaged his shoulders until he let out a big sigh, then led him quietly to the barn.

Ty seemed slightly more relaxed by the third day. Even though he hugged the back wall when I entered the stall, Ty stood very still and allowed me to slip a halter on without trying to move away. He stood like a gentleman in crossties while I quickly groomed him and picked manure out of his feet. When lifting the snaffle bit of the training bridle up to his mouth, I noticed a bizarre scar in the corner of Ty's lower left lip. The scar was faint, but it clearly was in the shape of an "x". Oddly, the *same* type of scar was present in the corner of his right lower lip! Oftentimes, bits will chafe or rub on this tender area of the mouth, but could *not* cause this type of lesion. Whatever happened to this horse had to have been intentional. I couldn't feel any scar tissue on the inside of the lips, and since the area appeared to be completely healed, I put the bridle on and carefully adjusted the cheek pieces.

Carefully gathering the reins, I slipped my left foot into the stirrup. With one smooth movement, I boosted myself onto Ty's back and settled softly into the saddle. Collecting the reins, I cued him to move forward. Without hesitation, he stepped out into a swift, ground-covering walk. After several rounds, I urged him gently into a trot. The elegant chestnut gelding responded immediately, accelerating into an astonishingly energetic and elevated trot. *Wow*, I thought, *what incredible power this horse has!* I couldn't help smiling as I felt the athleticism of this magnificent creature. Cautiously, I applied a little more rein pressure and brought Ty back to a walk.

As soon as I directed Ty to turn to the right, he became rigid and

14

refused to move either his head or neck. Forcing him to turn might cause Ty to rear up, which could result in him falling over backwards, pinning or crushing me as well as seriously injuring himself. Instead, I swung my right arm in a sweeping motion well away from his body to ease up pressure on the bars of his mouth. Ty moved hesitantly to the right, but with his head and neck held rigidly instead of bending. It reminded me of how a bus maneuvers a turn through an intersection. I cued Ty into a trot. This time, his body was so tense that the gait was short and choppy compared to the flowing, high-stepping movement he exhibited in the reverse direction.

Well, isn't this special, I fumed. *Poor horse has something wrong with its mouth and the solution is to get rid of him?* Lawrence probably had no clue there could be a physical cause for Ty's behavior, although the previous owner most likely *did* know.

Dr. Ben arrived early the next morning. He was a tall, big-framed man with a gruff voice. Ty immediately went into fear mode when he heard Dr. Ben, cowering and trembling at the back of the stall. The seasoned equine doctor took a minute to assess Ty before he attempted to enter the stall. Dr. Ben was affectionately known as "Gentle Ben" to a good number of his clients as he had a gentle and compassionate manner of working with skittish horses, despite his gravelly voice.

"Hey guy," Ben croaked, "can we take a peek?"

Dr. Ben patted the side of Ty's neck then massaged his withers and the top of his back until he was sure Ty was relaxed enough to begin the exam. Ben checked his back, all four legs and neck before attempting inspection of his mouth. Nothing abnormal was discovered. Ben moved slowly around Ty, rubbing his face and lips, then inserted several fingers in Ty's mouth, looking for clues to why he had the odd head tilt. Nothing out of the ordinary was found. Dr. Ben suggested taking an X-ray of his head to rule-out a more serious condition, such as infection or a tumor. I asked Dr. Ben as to why Ty had the criss-cross scars in the corners of his mouth. His answer shocked me.

"Well, I've seen this a few times with these Arab show horses," Ben explained. "Seems like a few unethical trainers will take a sharp knife or scalpel blade and make those cuts you're seeing."

"But why?" I quizzed. "What on earth do they do that for?"

"Think about it," Ben challenged, "you make the mouth sore, the horse doesn't lug on the bit. Keeps your English pleasure horses 'light' on the bit."

That made me angry. I had *never* heard of such a practice, and I couldn't fathom who would even *think* of doing something so inhumane! My stomach burned from the outrage I felt as I envisioned the process and the resultant pain and suffering Ty had endured. Mutilation of this fine creature for the purpose of financial gain was unbelievable in my mind.

"Ben, you've *got* to be kidding me. Really, seriously, this *happens?*"

Ben removed his cap, ran his hand over his balding head, and uttered, "Yep. Doesn't happen a lot because of the new ASHA rules. But you've got some trainers that will do it if they feel they can get away with it."

My heart went out to Ty. The poor horse. No wonder he was afraid and distrustful of humans! Most horses who suffer this type of abuse are marred emotionally for life. Some would become aggressive and dangerous. Others remained so frightened nothing could be done with them. Yet this good-natured, timid horse still allowed human interaction. He tried so hard to do his best when being ridden.

The next day, Dr. Ben called and asked me to come to the office to view the x-rays. "I've got something very interesting to show you," Ben stated.

Hurriedly, I headed to Ben's office. I was a first-year student in veterinary school and soaked up all of the interesting cases I could. Ben had the radiographs hanging on the brightly lit viewbox. He pointed to a white opacity that was about an inch long, lying parallel beneath the surface of Ty's right lower gumline.

"Here's your problem," Ben said confidently. "This is a blind wolf tooth. Since it's sideways instead of vertical, it can't erupt through the surface. Every time the bit comes in contact with this, it's sensitive enough to cause sharp pain. When you exert pressure on the rein, he protects himself from more pain by 'locking' his jaw. Once we do surgery to remove it, he should be fine."

Holy buckets, a horse was almost ruined because no one *took the time or cared to check it out*, I seethed. *Darn it, why do the animals have to suffer from human neglect or outright abuse? What kind of person would intentionally maim an animal with a knife to get it to hold its head higher? What other atrocities will I discover while I'm working with other animals?*

Dr. Ben must have noticed my pained facial expression. "The horse will be fine after he gets that tooth out. You'll be able to ride him again in a couple of weeks."

"You know, Ben, that's not my concern. I'm steaming mad because of the abuse this poor guy had to endure. It's just not right!"

"I hear you, but it's so hard to *catch* someone in the act. You're probably aware that Iowa has some of the most lax abuse and neglect laws in the country," Ben claimed.

"Uh, no, I didn't know that." I sighed as I sadly processed his words.

I did a little research that evening and found that Dr. Ben was right. Iowa was in the lowest tier of states for animal welfare. In the year 2015, Iowa would dive to number 49 out of 50 for states having the best animal protection laws. Interestingly, its bordering state, Illinois, would rank number one, according to the Animal Legal Defense Fund's annual year-end report. Iowa was assigned its unusually low rating because of an Ag-Gag law. This law was designed to silence whistleblowers revealing animal abuses on industrial farms. In essence, it would stop a person from recording, possessing, or distributing a video of the abuse. Years later, after graduating from veterinary school, I became a member of the Iowa Veterinary Medical Association's Animal Welfare committee and participated in several major abuse/neglect cases involving horses and other species. Not many veterinarians wanted to get involved with these cases and I felt a big responsibility to help the innocent creatures.

Dr. Ben dropped the bloody tooth extractor into the stainless steel pail filled with disinfectant solution, then held out his hand with the tiny vestigial of a tooth. "Here's your offender. Amazing how something this small can cause so much pain." The tooth was no longer than three-quarters of an inch, and only about as wide as a skewer stick. Ben slipped it into a plastic bag and handed it to me. "Make sure you show it to this horse's owner."

Two weeks later, I cautiously saddled up Ty and put him through his paces. Lawrence watched from the gate as Ty walked, trotted, and cantered gracefully and energetically around the arena both directions. There was absolutely no evidence of pain or discomfort, and the resistance on his right side was completely gone. Even though the mistreated gelding had recovered completely from his physical ailments, he still carried emotional trauma which necessitated special care from his handlers. He was especially nervous around men, and oftentimes I was the only person who could catch Ty when he was turned out. Eventually, Lawrence tired of having to walk on eggshells around his horse and put him up for sale.

I had grown quite fond of Ty and hated the thought of him being sold to a stranger. After negotiating a fair price, Lawrence signed over the papers to me.

Ty had his new "forever home."

Chapter 3
Ibn

Ibn danced around in the crossties as my daughter, Carrie, tightened the girth of the saddle in preparation for her riding lesson. The striking white Arabian gelding was her favorite lesson horse. His extreme intelligence challenged and sometimes intimidated his riders, but not Carrie. Her assertive personality and confidence in the saddle usually interrupted Ibn's attempts to be mischievous, transforming him into an obedient and responsive mount.

Carrie unsnapped the chain ties from Ibn's halter and led him into the arena. Ibn rolled the bit around in his mouth playfully as Carrie adjusted the girth for the last time. Ibn never stood still for very long, like a child with a short attention span. When she swung onto his back, Ibn pranced in anticipation.

"Carrie, make him walk!" Karen shouted from the middle of the arena. Karen was Carrie's instructor and also was the owner of the stable where Ibn had been born and raised. Karen had trained Ibn from the start, taking him from a winning halter horse to a seasoned western pleasure horse. She knew this gelding like the back of her hand. "Don't let him jig!" she commanded.

Ibn jogged along like a naughty little boy, testing the waters to see what he could get away with. Carrie immediately shortened the reins, settled her seat down firmly on his back, and asked him to walk. Ibn shook his head in defiance, then walked forward as asked. "That's much better." Karen's voice softened. One thing Karen couldn't tolerate was a student who didn't take charge of her horse from the very first step. Smart horses like Ibn would eventually take advantage of their riders, which could mean the difference between placing in a class or not, or possibly putting the rider in danger.

"Warm him up for a few minutes at a trot then we'll get started," Karen instructed. Carrie eased Ibn into an ultra-smooth jog trot, performing figure eights to limber up his body. After his muscles were warmed up, Karen coached Carrie how to perform flying lead changes. Actually, Ibn taught *Carrie* how—just stay out of his way and let him do them on his own! If Carrie attempted to cue him for the lead change, it appeared awkward and jumpy. So she learned to just sit tall and *look* in the direction she wanted him to go. Smooth as silk, Ibn completed the maneuver like a seasoned reining horse.

"Dang, girl, you did good!" Karen exclaimed. She walked over to the horse and rider team and squeezed Carrie's leg affectionately. Rarely did Karen get that excited over one of her student's accomplishments. Carrie tried to suppress a smile but she couldn't stop her face from beaming with joy at Karen's praise.

"Thanks, Karen. He's so easy to ride. Like I didn't even use my legs to cue him."

"I know," replied Karen, "but *you* put your *intent* out there. A lot of riders don't get that."

Carrie leaned over the saddle horn and patted Ibn affectionately on the neck. She was falling in love with this charismatic horse. Secretly, Carrie often fantasized what it would be like if Ibn were *hers*. Perhaps they would sail across an open field at breathtaking speed, or the two might tackle some challenging trails at some of the state parks. Most of all, Carrie dreamed of showing this beautiful, brilliant gelding. As a four-year old child, Carrie won her first blue ribbon in a large leadline class on one of Karen's Arabian mares. Her passion for riding continued to grow and flourish as a result of that initial experience.

Karen and I met for lunch a few days later. The two of us had become very good friends over the past several years, and getting together for a quick meal was a common event for us. As we sat down at our favorite booth, I sensed that Karen was stressed. Normally talkative and smiling, she was subdued and quiet.

"Hey, are you feeling alright?" I asked. "You look like something's wrong."

Karen cleared her throat and looked me intently in the eye. "I've got to sell some horses. I've been turning away people looking to board their horses because we're out of room. Jim seems to think we'd make more money boarding horses than raising them."

"Oh my, is that what *you* want to do?"

"You know me. Of course I don't", Karen grumbled. "I'd keep every one of them, but that just isn't feasible." The market for quality Arabian horses was starting a long, steady decline and prices had dropped dramatically in just the past year. Karen had been around horses for almost forty years. Except for her volunteer firefighter and first responder positions, horses were her life. Giving them up would be one of the most difficult things she had ever done.

"Ibn too?" I gulped. "You're putting him up for sale?"

"That's what I wanted to talk to you about today. He has to go too." Karen's face displayed the heaviness she felt having to re-home one of her favorite horses.

"Barb," said Karen seriously, "If I have to sell Ibn, I want him to go to someone who will love him, *use* him, and *keep* him. You remember what happened a few years ago when I got Ibn back after the girl who was showing him lost interest. I want a *forever home*. I know how much Carrie loves that horse and how well she gets along with him."

I reeled at Karen's suggestion. It *would* be wonderful to have this amazing horse in our animal family, but I also knew Ibn would be well out of our price range. I started to explain the finances, but Karen interrupted me. "Ibn is well past his prime for showing at the accredited shows. That means I can't begin to ask what he was worth ten years ago. Carrie could have a lot of fun taking him to 4H shows and local saddle club events. I'm only asking a thousand dollars for him. That's *your* price, so keep it quiet. And I would ask that you board him here at my stable, for as long as you can."

"Geesh, Karen, I can't believe my ears!" I exclaimed. "I'm so excited!! But I'll have to run it by the other half first, so can you give me until tomorrow to make a decision?"

"No problem, just let me know as soon as you can."

I was a little nervous about approaching Fred with the purchase of another horse. Although he had been raised around his dad's Saddlebreds and liked horses, he was very money-conscious. There would be another monthly boarding bill to pay, in addition to farrier work, extra tack and equipment, and riding lessons. I would have to convince Fred that Carrie would be in a great environment, that she would learn responsibility for someone besides herself, and that there was a substantial amount of work involved with horses. Fortunately, Fred agreed to the purchase with the condition that Carrie take on a part-time job to help pay for Ibn's upkeep.

Karen was thrilled to hear the news. It was a huge relief to know Ibn would have his forever home with us. She was so excited that she planned a party for Carrie at her stable the following weekend. There were cupcakes, chips, and pop for the kids, and carrots, apples, and peppermint treats for the horses. Ibn's favorite snack was carrots. He simply could *not* get enough of them. As the kids were filling their plates with goodies, Ibn reminded them he needed carrots by scraping the inside wall of his stall with a front foot. Soon the bag of carrots was gone.

Carrie stepped inside his stall so we could get some pictures taken. Ibn, feeling deprived of additional carrots, stuck out his tongue, turned his head toward his new owner, and let a long string of saliva speckled with tiny orange chunks of carrot drip onto the back of Carrie's neck.

"Ugh! Ibbbbbbbbbnnnnnn!" she wailed, grabbing a napkin to wipe the goo from her hair. An explosion of laughter from everyone caused Carrie's face to turn a deep red from embarrassment. However, the young teenager was much too happy with her new horse to let it dampen her spirits.

Chapter 4
The Accident

We moved Tysheyn to Karen's stable, Whispering Oaks, after purchasing Ibn. The two horses had adjacent box stalls and a large outdoor pen for daytime exercise. They quickly became best friends, often engaging in mutual back scratching or mock fighting by nipping at each other's face and head. Ty warmed up rapidly to Karen and the group of soft-hearted riding students. The kids had been instructed to go slowly around him since he had been previously mishandled, and they responded kindly and lovingly, stopping frequently to pet him and offer treats. Ty was extraordinarily docile around the youngsters. When offered a carrot, he would stand a few feet away and stretch his neck forward to reach timidly for the tasty tidbit. His lips would quiver in anticipation, then he would slip his lips around the carrot and gently remove it from the kid's hand.

The following winter turned out to be excessively cold and snowy. Drifts piled up in the outdoor pens and around the barn doors, making it impossible to turn horses out. The indoor arena was the only available place to exercise the horses so everyone took turns letting their horses out. Because temperatures were well below freezing, Karen was unable to water the arena floor, and it rapidly became dry and dusty.

Carrie and I drove to the stable one afternoon to let the "boys" out. When Ibn heard Carrie's voice, he started impatiently striking his front foot against the stall door. The sharp *rap, rap, rap* annoyed a mare directly across from Ibn. The irritated horse lunged toward the front of her stall with ears flat against her head, then hopped up and down on her rear legs several times. Her behavior didn't faze Ibn a bit. He continued striking the door until Carrie flung it open and demanded that he stop. Caught in the act, Ibn sullenly retreated toward the back of his stall.

"Wow, they look bored," I noted. "Let's get them out so they can stretch their legs."

Ibn pranced in anticipation as Carrie led the horses down the aisle. As soon as the lead ropes were unsnapped, they exploded into motion, galloping as fast and as hard as possible. Ty ran so hard that he almost slammed chest-first into the pipe gate at the opposite end of the arena. Ibn reared, spun, then raced across the middle of the ring, sliding to a stop inches away from his buddy. The horses paused momentarily, snorting loudly. With tails curled up over their backs, they took off again on a dead run. A grey, powdery cloud formed as the horses stirred up the dry arena floor, becoming thicker by the second as the horses continued to run.

Carrie and I escaped from the arena when the horses started their frantic sprinting. The dust cloud became so dense it was impossible to see them. Suddenly, there was a loud thud, then complete silence. I strained to see through the cloudy film as Carrie ran into the arena, terrified that something bad had happened. Carrie screamed, *"Mom! They're down!"*

I bounded through the gate and took off in the direction of Carrie's voice. As the dust cleared, Ty scrambled to his feet. Ibn was stretched out on his left side, eerily quiet. Carrie kneeled over him, crying as she stroked his head and begged him to get up. The two horses had collided head-on, unable to see the other as they raced around in the haze. Ibn made a feeble attempt to raise his head off of the ground, then groaned and let it fall back onto the ground.

"Carrie!! Run out to the truck and get my vet bag!!" I commanded. I had a sinking feeling as I mouthed the words to my daughter. My big concern was that Ibn had sustained a broken neck. Neck fractures in horses are very serious and usually result in a poor to grave prognosis. Carrie returned seconds later, with my medical bag carelessly slung over her shoulder. "Mom, is he going to be *okay?"* Carrie gasped with panic in her voice.

"Honey, give me a minute to check him out!" I replied. I carefully assessed Ibn's vital signs—heart rate, respiratory rate, gum color, and pupillary reflexes. Except for higher-than-normal breaths per minute, his vitals were good. I attributed his increase in breathing to lying on his side or possibly pain. Next, I carefully palpated all four legs for broken bones. So far, so good, I thought.

Ibn was blinking and watching me as I examined him. To finish the exam, he would need to be upright. "Come on, buddy, let's get up," I encouraged. I nudged him on the rump gently with the toe of my boot. Ibn rolled up onto his chest, but made no attempt to stand. I allowed him to rest for a few moments, then urged him to get up again. Still, Ibn refused to move. "Carrie, get me a carrot. *Please*. There should be some in the lounge."

Carrie bolted toward the rider's lounge and returned with a bag of carrots.

I snapped a carrot in two and Ibn perked up immediately. "Come on, buddy, you gotta *get up* to get your treat," I teased. "You can do it!" I coaxed, waving a piece of Ibn's favorite treat in front of his nose. He tried to grab it from me, but I swiftly retracted my hand. *Not just yet, buddy.*

The temptation of a crunchy fresh carrot was just too much for Ibn. He valiantly thrust his forelegs out in front of him, then with one mighty push from his rear legs, stood upright. He was a sorry sight as he swayed sideways like he'd had a few too many beers, with his head and neck held at a low angle. The left side of his body was covered in dirt and sand from lying on the ground, and his mane and tail were a dirty grey from dust. Ibn seized the carrot from my fingers and chewed slowly on it.

I took the other piece of carrot and held it off to Ibn's right side. He turned his head and neck without hesitation. Then I did the same on Ibn's left side. Again, he followed my hand with ease. I breathed a hesitant sigh of relief, because if Ibn had a neck fracture, he most likely would not be able to or would refuse to move it. However, he could have sustained a pretty nasty concussion, I surmised. Although there were no scrapes, cuts, or abrasions on his head, it was a possibility based on Ibn's weakness and incoordination.

Concerned that a dangerous pocket of fluid might develop in Ibn's skull, I administered emergency drugs intravenously. Within a few minutes, Ibn's eyes appeared clearer and he seemed steadier on his feet. Carrie carefully led her injured buddy back to his stall, then went to work making an extra deep bed of shavings so he could comfortably lie down.

Over the next several days, Ibn continued to recuperate. I consulted with one of the doctors at the Iowa State Veterinary College just to be on the safe side. The attending veterinarian advised me to continue corticosteroid injections for the next three days. The dosage that was recommended surprised me, but the clinician was confident that the higher amount was well-tolerated by most horses.

After another week, Ibn was better but he still carried his neck a little lower than normal and at a slight angle to the side. I decided to make an appointment at Iowa State College of Veterinary Medicine's Large Animal Hospital to have a specialist assess Ibn. He was far too precious to Carrie and me to not know if he needed additional treatment.

Dr. B, the clinician who was assigned Ibn's case, gave Ibn a thorough examination. She carefully checked his reflexes, his movement, and his eyesight. Everything seemed fine.

"Does he like treats?" Dr. B asked.

"Oh yes," I laughed, "if he refuses a treat, there's definitely something wrong with him."

"Okay then," Dr. B smiled, "let's see what he does with these." She pulled out several molasses horse treats from her pocket. Standing on tiptoes, Dr. B stretched her arm high in the air over Ibn's head, with one of the treats in her palm. The irresistible scent hit Ibn's nostrils, and he responded by raising his head as high as he could to take the tasty tidbit. Next, the specialist knelt down and held a treat between Ibn's front feet, causing him to stretch his neck all the way to the ground. Then she held her hand by Ibn's right shoulder, then to the his left, checking to see how far he could bend to each side. Dr. B giggled as Ibn chomped greedily on his snacks. "Well, I don't see anything wrong with his neck and shoulder mobility. But let's take some radiographs and just make sure there's nothing I'm missing."

The radiographs of Ibn's neck were completely normal, so Ibn was discharged with instructions to start light exercise and to continue the corticosteroids. "I'm pretty conservative when I give steroid therapy," I explained. "I've never given this high of a dose and I'm a little uneasy about it."

Dr. B confidently replied, "We frequently use up to five times the amount you've been giving with no ill effects. Since I'm suspicious that he has some lingering nerve inflammation, I'd continue with treatment for another three days. He should be fine after that. Just go slow with his rehabilitation, alright?"

We shook hands and I thanked Dr. B for her time and expertise.

"You've sure got a beautiful horse there, Dr. Lembke," the specialist remarked. "It was my pleasure working with him. His passion for treats made my exam easier," she laughed.

One week later, Carrie was leading Ibn back to the barn from his outdoor pen when she noticed that he was limping ever so slightly on his right front foot. *That's odd*, she thought, because Ibn had been fine that morning. Carrie picked Ibn's foot out with a hoof pick and didn't find anything such as a rock or piece of metal that might have gotten wedged in the crevices of his hoof. Carrie called me and explained the situation. I instructed her to apply a light application of liniment, thinking that maybe he twisted his fetlock, and promised Carrie I would check Ibn in the morning.

The next day, Ibn was lame on *both* front feet. He walked gingerly down the cement aisle way as I watched how he placed his heels down a fraction of a second before the rest of his foot hit the ground. Alarmed, I laid my fingers over the arteries that supplied the majority of blood to the foot. Normally, there wouldn't be any pulse. But Ibn had strong, bounding pulses, signaling significant inflammation within the feet. *Son of a gun*, I thought, *he's got laminitis. Not good. Not good at all!* I made a quick checklist of everything that could be causing his feet to flare up, and the only thing that made any sense was the steroid injections. Corticosteroids, in horses, can cause a painful foot condition if the horse is somehow predisposed to steroid sensitivity. There was nothing in Ibn's recent past, like diet change, that could be a trigger—except for the drugs to ease his inflammation.

So new therapies were started to reduce the danger of more complications from the laminitis. Ibn was confined to a heavily bedded stall until the pulses in his feet subsided. I knew from my experience with many cases of laminitis that it could take weeks, or even months, for the foot to heal, provided the horse responded to treatment. The condition causes severe inflammation in the laminae, or connective tissues, that hold the coffin bone in place in the hoof. If the inflammation and increased pressure inside the hoof capsule don't resolve, the coffin bone can become displaced at an angle in the hoof that can cause permanent lameness. The worst case scenario is where the bone actually "sinks" toward the sole of the foot, necessitating euthanasia.

Fortunately, Ibn responded well to the quick and aggressive treatment. In less than a week, Ibn was able to return to his outdoor pen with Ty, where they happily spent the daytime hours scratching each other's backs and bickering over whose hay pile was tastier.

Chapter 5
The Downhill Slide

During the next few years, Carrie and Ibn were an inseparable team, competing in local saddle club and 4H shows. Ibn was known affectionately to saddle club members as "The White Arab." He was usually the only Arabian at the shows, and won numerous classes in Trail, Western Horsemanship, Western Pleasure, and Halter. Occasionally, Carrie would enter him in some of the games like barrel racing and pole bending. Ibn was incredibly fast, and the faster he could go, the better he performed.

Every few months it seemed as if Ibn was slightly tender on his feet. Usually the discomfort started right after his feet were trimmed and had his shoes replaced. The farrier didn't see anything out of the ordinary, so I wasn't overly concerned. Giving Ibn a few days off from riding normally fixed the problem.

The following summer, Carrie won the title of "Black Hawk Creek Saddle Club Senior Queen," qualifying her for the prestigious Iowa Rodeo Queen contest at the state fair. I had no idea what a big deal the contest was, although other attendees had told me it was one of the most popular events. It was true. The indoor pavilion was packed to the limit with spectators at least an hour beforehand. Vendors selling popcorn and soda fought their way through crowded bleachers. Photographers from all over the state had equipment set up around the outside railing of the arena, and media crews were stationed on a platform high above the arena, set to capture the event on live television.

That evening, temperatures hovered in the high eighties. The air was oppressive when combined with the humidity. At least there was a southerly breeze as the contestants warmed up their horses in the outdoor arena adjoining the pavilion. Karen helped Carrie make some last minute adjustments to her chaps, then gave her a hug and boosted her into the saddle. "Go get 'em, kid!" she said as she squeezed Carrie's hand. "You can do it. Just remember to cue him lightly into a canter when you start your queen salute. Then let him rip. We don't want him bucking, right?"

Carrie nodded. "Got it, Coach. Thanks."

Karen had offered to accompany Carrie and me to the contest since my dear dad passed away unexpectedly two weeks prior. Karen knew I was not handling the loss well and needed some strong emotional support. Fred was distant and unemotional toward me after Dad's death, leaving me feeling abandoned and alone in my sorrow. Fighting back tears as I gave one last "high five" to Carrie, I left the warmup area to find my mom and the rest of the family in the bleachers.

The heat inside of the arena was stifling. Immediately, I was concerned for Ibn's welfare. As soon as I located my family and said hellos and hugged everyone, I hurried back to the warmup arena where Carrie and Ibn were seeking shade under one of the large maple trees. I noticed Ibn was already damp with sweat.

"Carrie, you've got at least twenty horses in your class. Make sure you're one of the last, if not the last, in the ring. I don't want Ibn in that hot arena any longer than necessary. I'll be here at the gate when you come out. We'll unsaddle and sponge him down right away," I instructed as I scurried to the barn to grab a pail of cool water and a sponge.

By the time I got back to the pavilion, the arena bleachers were completely filled. My brother had tried saving me a seat near them, but someone insisted on taking it. The only place I could watch the competition was from the entryway. I had to stand on tiptoes to see.

One by one, the beautifully adorned contestants jogged into the arena on their impeccably groomed and polished horses. The crowd erupted with booming applause and hooting as their favorites passed in front of them. The noise startled several horses, but the riders were skilled enough to get their horse under control. After the horse and rider teams were judged at a walk, jog, and lope, they lined up in the middle of the arena. Then one at a time, riders galloped their horse at full speed around the perimeter of the arena, saluting the audience. Spectators stomped their feet on the metal bleachers, shouted, screamed, and clapped as they flew by.

Ibn performed a perfectly executed sliding stop, then Carrie expertly backed him parallel to the judge. They had an exceptional ride that earned them an impressive third place in the large, competitive class. I watched Ibn's sides heaving from exertion, and his normally white, shiny coat was dark grey from excessive sweat. The insides of his flaring nostrils were alarmingly red. I tried to push my way through the crowd to signal Carrie to dismount and loosen the girth on the saddle, but she had already sensed that her horse might be in danger of hyperthermia. Instead of waiting to accept her award, she slid out of the saddle, unbuckled the girth, led her horse out of the arena. Karen and I worked quickly to remove the saddle and pad and begin sponging cool water over Ibn's neck, forehead, and back. Once outside in the evening breeze, he cooled off quickly.

"Mom, he was *so* geared in the arena!" Carrie exclaimed. "I could hardly hold him back! Is he going to be okay?"

"Oh, I think so, especially after he has a few hours to rest before we haul him home. You had an awesome ride, Carrie; so proud of you! Now get back inside and accept your award." I let out a big sigh of relief now that the event was over, grateful that Carrie got through it safely and Ibn was responding well to the tepid bath and summer breezes.

Fairground regulations prohibited the horses from being allowed to stay overnight. It was close to ten o'clock and we still had a two-hour drive home. Yet I wanted to make sure Ibn was fully cooled out and comfortable before we left. Enclosed horse trailers, even with screens for ventilation, can become uncomfortably warm. We finally pulled out at midnight, assured that Ibn would have a pleasant ride home.

A few days later, the tenderness in Ibn's front feet came back. This time, it was more pronounced. Nothing had changed in his routine, except for the stress of competing in the Rodeo Queen contest. I administered the regular medications to help with pain and inflammation, and within a few days, he appeared normal.

When Ibn started to grow his winter coat in late August, it hit me like a brick wall as to what was going on. Laminitis—excessive sweating, inability to shed hair properly or a thicker haircoat in general—

all led up to a diagnosis of Cushing's syndrome. Bloodwork confirmed the diagnosis. I was crushed when my suspicions were confirmed. *How do I tell Carrie? My God, Ibn has been her rock for the past few years! Please Lord, help me!*

Carrie listened quietly as I explained what the disease could do to her horse. The most serious complication would be continued flareups of laminitis which could eventually cripple him for life. He could develop liver dysfunction, systemic infections, a heart condition, high blood pressure, and a list of other less serious illnesses. He would most likely have to be shaved down in the summer, as Cushing's syndrome horses often don't shed their winter hair, making them exceptionally hot in the summer months. I carefully broke the news to my daughter that he should be permanently retired from the show ring, as the stress (both mental and physical) would be too great on his body.

Surprisingly, Carrie accepted the news with minimal emotion. "Mom, I really don't care if I can't show anymore. Look at all the things I've done with him. He's getting too old to be competitive anyways. I still love and care for him a lot, but…I don't need to ride him." Carrie turned sideways in her chair and stared out the kitchen window. "He's been a great horse." Her chin quivered as she attempted to hide unexpected tears.

"Honey, I'm going to do everything possible to keep him going, but there are no guarantees," I explained. I discovered that several half-siblings and at least one full sibling to Ibn suffered from Cushing's-like symptoms, leading me to believe there could be a genetic component involved. At the time, drugs to treat Cushing's were just being developed, and unfortunately, were still in the experimental stages. Treatment would be aimed at supportive care.

Even with my assurance that we would do everything possible to keep Ibn happy and healthy, Carrie subconsciously started to detach from her best friend. It was a protective mechanism she developed to keep herself from getting hurt. She couldn't bear the thought of losing him, despite my encouragement to keep a positive attitude. Ibn sensed the change in Carrie's demeanor too. He worked extra hard to cheer her up by performing silly antics like sticking his tongue out at her and rubbing his head up and down on her back when she picked manure out of his stall. Sometimes his actions caused her to cry; other times he elicited a laugh out of *his* girl.

Over the course of a few months, Ibn held his own. The episodic laminitis was managed well with anti-inflammatory drugs and careful attention to his nutritional status. Although he would never perform as a show horse again, Ibn was still a favorite at Karen's stable with the kids, loving every second of attention from his admirers.

Chapter 6
Stormy Bey

A year after Ibn had been retired, I received a call from a long-time acquaintance and horse trainer, Deb Johnson. "Hey Barb, I know it's been a while since we saw each other. Hope all is going well with you," she stated.

I was curious as to why she was calling me. "Yes, everything is fine, thank you. What can I do for you?"

"Well, I have a horse that's for sale and your name came to mind."

"Deb, I'm not looking—"

"You might be very interested when I tell you who it is," she interrupted. "You remember Lawrence Brown, right? This horse was born and raised on his farm."

"Oh yes, I know Lawrence. I bought Tysheyn from him about ten years ago."

"That's right," Deb recalled. "You still have Ibn, too, don't you?"

"We do, but he's pretty much retired because of lameness issues. Carrie is taking it okay even though she would love to be able to finish out her last season in youth competition."

Deb described the situation with the horse that needed a new home. After purchasing the gelding from the Browns for a hefty amount of money, the buyer's thirteen-year old daughter started showing him at local and regional Arabian shows, always staying "in the ribbons." A few years later, her parents divorced, and the teenage rider turned to drinking and hanging with the wrong crowd. The horse was no longer a priority with the family. The mother still paid the boarding, veterinary, and farrier bills, but no one had ridden the gelding for over a year.

"Okay, Deb, who *is* this horse?" I asked impatiently.
"Stormy Bey. I believe you remember him."

Of course I remembered him! He was such a sweetheart. I first saw Stormy as a yearling when I was completing a summer internship with Lawrence's veterinarian. We had been pregnancy checking mares on Lawrence and Karla's farm. Lawrence was excited to show off his new crop of foals. He led us to a beautiful, large pasture that ten mares, their babies, and a few yearlings shared. They had lots of sunshine, plenty of room to play and socialize. The mares were amazingly accepting as we walked amongst the group. None of the mares felt threatened or overly protective of their offspring. The babies loved checking us over with their soft muzzles. One persistent little guy kept nibbling Dr. Ben's coveralls with his tiny teeth.

Lawrence directed our attention to a beautiful, dark bay yearling toward the back of the herd. He was standing timidly behind his mother, a few yards away from the others. His large, soft brown eyes immediately tugged at my heart. With our eyes locked in a gaze, the inquisitive young gelding took a step toward me. Then he took another. The handsome young horse waited until I stretched out my hand to invite him to come closer. Hesitantly, he approached. He sniffed my hand and waited quietly while I moved close to his side. He stood politely while I stroked his shoulder and neck. For whatever reason, I felt a strong connection to him, even though it was the first time I'd laid eyes on him.

Lawrence and Karla's foals would start their show training after they reached a year of age. The Browns bred their horses to make money, and horse shows were a way for an owner to advertise his or her horses. Winning a class, especially a championship, increases its value whether it's in breeding fees or sale price. It was the trainer's responsibility to bring out the best in a horse through their training program.

Sometimes the training is intense. Sometimes it could be considered by some as inhumane. Reputable trainers would see to it that their clients' animals were treated fairly and humanely, although some of the training practices were nowhere close to being "kind". Because there was oftentimes a lot of money at stake, Lawrence encouraged his trainer to "do what it takes" to win.

The last time I'd seen Stormy was when he was in a two-year old halter futurity at a large Arabian show. There was quite a bit of money involved in the futurity, and I was eager to see how Stormy would place in this class of exquisitely beautiful geldings. He was a gorgeous deep bay with sturdy, straight legs and a beautiful head that exemplified the Arabian breed. His coat glistened under the bright arena lights from the intense grooming and prepping with special sprays and polishes. Halter horses are judged on their conformation, beauty, and movement. Each handler enters the arena running alongside his horse, controlling it with it a thin patent leather strap attached to a very dainty halter. After they make their entrance, the horse is put into a particular stance that shows off its physique. The judge then examines each horse closely, assessing any structural defects as well as its unique strengths.

Because the standard for halter horses is to be extremely animated when they enter the ring, there are a few tricks to the trade that I had heard of from various "whistleblowers." One method is to "ginger" the horse's anus with a special compound that irritates the sensitive rectal tissue, causing the horse to hold its tail excessively high. The other method of exciting the horse is to take it into a stall and crack whips around—and unfortunately sometimes *on*—the horse to create a wide-eyed, frantic attitude so when the horse entered the arena, it would move more boldly. Since the advent of whip rules sanctioned by the International Arabian Horse Association, the practice of physical contact with the whips has been banned. If a horse entering the arena was found to have welts or mark from a whip, it would immediately be disqualified from competition.

On the night of the Gold Star Futurity, I joined Lawrence and Karla in the bleachers. At the time, I knew very little about all of the dirty secrets behind the scenes. I was aware of the whip rule that was in force, and each horse would be inspected for whip marks as it stood along the rail for the judge's initial analysis. As each beautiful Arabian gelding entered the arena, the crowd cheered for their favorites. Twelve horses were entered in this section of the futurity, but so far, only eleven were in the ring. *Where was Stormy Bey?* Lawrence nervously glanced at the neon timer above the announcer's stand. There was a two-minute rule: from the first call for the class, all horses had 120 seconds to enter the ring or the gate would be closed and latecomers would be barred from entering. The neon timer above the announcer's stand read 1:46. The clock ticked away as Lawrence and Karla waited anxiously. With just a few seconds remaining, Stormy and his trainer raced into the arena. Stormy was stunningly gorgeous, with his long black tail flowing freely and his neck arched majestically with head held high. Once in position, the judge walked around Stormy, scribbling notes on his pad as he examined the conformation of his legs. When the judge reached Stormy's right hip, he stopped and signaled for the show steward to approach. (A show steward is the "show cop", meaning he or she can eliminate or disqualify a horse if it has been proven to be drugged, if the horse is obviously lame, or other sanctioned rules have been broken.) The judge ran his hand slowly over the top of the Stormy's right hip. The two officials and the trainer were locked in discussion for several minutes before the judge returned to the center of the arena to make his final placings. The show steward escorted Stormy and his handler out of the ring. Lawrence leaped to his feet and immediately headed toward the barn to investigate what had happened.

Stormy Bey was disqualified for four *six-inch long welts* on his right hip from being whipped. I was livid—not at the rules because the rules would hopefully prevent more abuse like this—but at the trainer, who I had respected and held to a high ethical standard. It seemed so unfair to take a beautiful, mild-mannered creature and subject him to this kind of abuse. My heart bled for him! Lawrence and Karla were so upset that they hauled Stormy back home that same evening, even though he had been entered in other halter classes. Later, Lawrence confided in me that he felt Stormy wasn't happy at the trainer's facility. Two nights in a row, Stormy had somehow wriggled out of expensive winter blankets. He destroyed them by urinating and defecating on them, then ripping them to shreds by stomping incessantly on the fabric. It was as if he was saying, "Screw all of you! Get me out of here!"

"Deb, I have always loved that horse. Like I said, though, we're not really looking for a new horse and I'm sure Stormy's asking price is way beyond our budget," I sighed, as an immediate image of what my husband's face would look like if I mentioned buying another horse.

Deb replied, "Oh, they're only asking $1,200. They just want to get him sold as quickly as possible. Stormy really needs some attention.

He's only nine years old so he has some great time ahead of him. Are you interested at all?"

I was completely shocked at the low price since the Browns had sold him for close to ten thousand dollars. "Can you give me twenty-four hours to make a decision?" I asked hesitantly.

"Sure, no problem. But let me know as soon as you can because I may have another buyer for him."

I cringed at the idea of Stormy going to someone else. There was just *something* about the gentle gelding that got to me. I knew, though, that convincing Fred to purchase another horse would be no easy task.

That evening, Fred was dozing off in front of the television as I arrived home from after a stressful evening of after-hours emergency calls. It was only 9:30 but I could tell by the empty tumbler sitting next to his recliner that he'd had a few Jack Daniels & Cokes. This conversation could either be neutral or volatile, depending on his mood. But I didn't want to wait. I promised Deb I would call her back the next morning with an answer.

"Hey, I'm home."

"Yeah, what's up," he mumbled.

"If you're awake enough, I want to talk to you about something."

"Go ahead, I'm listening," he replied as he lifted the glass to his lips and sucked out the last few drops.

I told Fred about the phone call from Deb and how Stormy ended up at her farm. I brought up the fact that his asking price was incredibly cheap compared to what it had been originally. I even told him about the tears Carrie shed when she had to retire Ibn for good. Surprisingly, he said, "Go for it."

"So I have your approval on this? Are you sure?" I questioned apprehensively.

"Yeah." He leaned back in the recliner and closed his eyes. "Carrie should have a decent horse for her last year."

Now I couldn't tell if he was being sincere or if there was a hint of sarcasm in his voice. But I tried to remain optimistic that Fred's true feelings had surfaced and he really did want Carrie to have a dependable and healthy show horse.

The next morning, Fred informed me that I could purchase

Stormy *if* Deb would come down to one thousand dollars. I told him it wasn't up her to decide; the owners would have to approve the offer.

"So, tell your friend we're offering a thousand bucks, and no more." My heart sank, worried that our offer would be rejected. But I knew that if I pushed the issue, my husband might flip and say no to Stormy's purchase, after all.

I nervously picked up the phone and called Deb after Fred left for work. "Hey Deb, we're very interested in buying Stormy. I have to tell you though, that I can't offer you the full amount you're asking. If the owners can part with him for a thousand, we have a deal."

Later that afternoon, Deb called me back and said the owners accepted the offer. I was ecstatic, anxious to welcome the *beautiful boy* to our family. Stormy Bey now had his "forever home."

Chapter 7
Unrest

A year had passed since Stormy joined the family. Although it was wonderful having the horses at Karen's stable, the boarding fee for three horses was becoming a burden. I thought the best thing would be to look for our own horse acreage. My decision was solidified when Karen announced that she had filed for divorce and the barn would most likely be going to her husband. I liked Jim, but I had a gut feeling that things wouldn't be the same if Karen lost the barn in the divorce settlement.

One evening, as I was searching through the real estate for sale section of the paper, one particular ad jumped out:

Just listed - hobby horse farm - 5 acres of rolling timber and pasture - seven-stall metal barn with '50 x 100' indoor arena - older ranch house with large family room and walkout basement - beautiful setting - owner anxious to sell... The acreage was located just across the county line, which meant that property taxes would be much less than what we were presently paying. With seven stalls and an indoor arena in the barn, I figured we could take on a few boarders as well to offset the mortgage payment. Excitedly, I scribbled notes down so I had all of the details before I mentioned anything to Fred about it.

That evening, I carefully approached him about the acreage. As no surprise to me, Fred came up with all kinds of excuses as to why he didn't want to consider it: can't afford it, too long of a commute to work, too much work associated with an acreage, don't know anybody in Butler County, etc. I pointed out to him that property taxes would be at least half of what we were presently paying. There would be no more boarding bills. I showed him how much we could reduce the mortgage payment by if I boarded a few horses and took on a few riding students.

Fred reluctantly agreed to look at the property.

I knew he was not enthusiastic at all about moving to the country, but I secretly reasoned that if our relationship went south, the horses, Carrie, and I could live comfortably. I also knew the great majority of the upkeep, such as lawn mowing, weeding, landscaping, cleaning stalls, and fixing fence would be my responsibility. I hoped Fred would eventually enjoy rural life and its many positive benefits.

Whether it was guilt at how he had been treating me, a revelation that country life would be "okay," or the fact he'd be saving money by moving to the country, Fred agreed to look at the acreage. Although the house needed major updating, along with a few minor exterior repairs, the setting was beautiful and the horse barn was fairly new. There was even a place to park my mobile veterinary clinic inside the barn.

"I don't know," Fred said, in his you-make-the-decision-so-I-can-criticize-you-later voice. "It's a long drive to work. The place is on a gravel road. It's gonna be hard on the vehicles. And what are you going to do with your mobile clinic? Drive it on the snowed-in road in the winter time?"

"Okay. For starters, it's only twenty minutes to your work place. I drive all over anyway, so wherever I end up doesn't matter. Yes, we live on gravel, but it's only a few miles to a state highway. The amount of money we'll save on property taxes and not having to pay for boarding horses will more than make up for the wear and tear on the vehicles. And if you remember, I was snowed in for days in Cedar Falls, because I never had an indoor shelter for the clinic. It was super hard to keep everything from freezing even though the unit was plugged in. Carrie only has one year left of school, and she has just a bit further to drive to get to Janesville. Once she's done, she can decide to stay here or get her own apartment."

Fred rubbed his chin thoughtfully. "You have some good arguments. But the house needs a lot of work. How are we going to afford that?"

"We can do a little at a time. I can live with minimal updates. You know I've never been a material person."

"Yeah." He shot me a glance that made me cringe. The smirk and the tone of voice reeked of sarcasm. "So we live in a dump so the horses can live in a palace."

41

"Come on, Fred," I retorted. "The house is not a 'dump'. Eventually, we can replace the carpeting and get some nicer flooring in the bathroom and kitchen. A few coats of paint on the garage door and the bedroom walls will make a big difference. The roof is good, furnace is new, and we'll have a great view out of those huge bay windows in the living room." I waited a few seconds to see what he would rebut me with but Fred remained quiet. "You were the first one to mention that the horses were costing too much where they are now. There really isn't anything in Black Hawk County that we can afford. If you want to look around, that's fine, but I'm telling you what I've come across is way out of our budget."

Fred grudgingly agreed to make an offer on the acreage. It was quite a bit lower than the asking price, but after just one counteroffer, the property became ours.

Ty, Ibn, and Stormy thought the acreage was the greatest place on earth. They had full run of the entire pasture during the day, and in the evening had roomy box stalls to relax in. The very first thing all three boys would do when first let out in the wee hours of the morning was to race down the hill to the west. Ibn was always first, then Ty was a close second with Stormy at his heels. All three would buck and jump a few times before they settled down for some serious grazing. Stormy was fascinated with deer that came up to the east fence line. On several occasions, I witnessed him touching noses with one of the does. Ty and Ibn were leery of those strange creatures that lurked in the thick timber and kept their distance.

The first summer at the new acreage was incredibly hot and humid. The barn had good ventilation, with full-size, sliding doors on the west side and another adjacent to the indoor arena. However, the house, lacking central air conditioning, was unbearably hot, even with big shade trees surrounding it and ceiling fans in every room. Tempers commonly flared. Fred accused me that I had been negligent at the real estate closing. "I don't know how *you* could have missed that!"

"I *didn't* miss it, if you'll remember!" I hissed back. "You told the realtor it wasn't any big deal, we'd get central air *later.*"

"Yeah? Well, I don't remember *that,*" he grumbled.

I thought to myself, *Well, I'm the one who's really suffering in the heat, not him.* Fred held an 8 - 4:30 desk job, then headed directly for the YMCA, where he worked out until 7:30 p.m. By the time he got home and fixed himself a few cocktails, it was time to turn in. We had a small window air conditioner in our bedroom, so it was fairly comfortable while sleeping. I felt like I was between a rock and a hard spot. *Darned if I do, darned if I don't.* I made the decision that evening to take money from my business account and get central air installed.

As the summer progressed, I spent most of my evenings with the horses. They were great therapy, sensing when I was stressed. One particularly difficult day left me physically and emotionally drained. It started when I received a phone call from one of my best equine clients at 5:27 a.m. I immediately sensed the shakiness and urgency in her voice. "Barb, you have to come right over. One of our mares has a foot that is just hanging by the skin." *What? Am I really hearing this or am I still asleep in the middle of a nightmare?* I knew this client would never call with something trivial. If she said the foot was attached by only skin, I knew it was bad. "I'll be right there, Pat," I assured her as I flew into my veterinary coveralls.

I witnessed one of the worst injuries I'd ever seen in equine practice. The mare, a gorgeous and very expensive Peruvian Paso, had somehow gotten one of its front legs wedged solidly between the automatic waterer and the wall of the stall. During the struggle to free her leg, the mare fell, breaking the lower part of her cannon bone. She continued to struggle, stripping almost all of the skin from the bones, tendons, and ligaments. Her hoof was literally hanging by shreds of skin. The bedding and side of the stall were plastered with fresh blood. Pat's husband, Dan, discovered the mare when he went down to feed the horses. He immediately called in his construction crew, who were already loading trucks and trailers for the day's work. They were able to cut a hole in the wall to free the mare's leg. But it was much too late. I arrived fifteen minutes later to find four sturdy, grown men weeping as they stroked the mare's trembling body. She was in shock and excruciating pain. The only "treatment" I could offer the mare was an injection of euthanasia solution. I put my arms around each of the men in an attempt to offer some comfort as tears spilled down their cheeks.

My day didn't end there. I got an angry call from a new client that had wanted me to x-ray a four-year old horse he had sold. The buyers had previously purchased a horse with significant arthritis in one of the bones of its feet and were leery of purchasing another without having it x-rayed first. The client's adult son was at the farm to help me hold the horse while I took radiographs. I noticed several empty tubes of Bute, a veterinary paste that kills pain, lying around the barn. The son brought the horse up from its stall and I took several pictures of the front feet. I noticed some odd "rings" in the hoof wall, but the son assured me the horse had never been lame. After developing the films, I was shocked at what I saw. The coffin bones had "sunk" inside of the hoof capsules, a huge red flag for severe laminitis. It also explained the layers of rings in the hoof wall. The client had wanted me to focus on the navicular bone (to rule out navicular syndrome), but the abnormalities in the coffin bones were obvious—and serious.

I called the number the client had given me, but nobody answered. He had been adamant that I give him a call right away because the buyers were coming to pick up the horse that evening if the x-rays were normal. No one left me an alternate phone number, so I drove back out to the farm. The son was still there, so I held the radiograph films up to the sunlight and explained what I had found. He told me his dad had to make a quick trip out of town but to go ahead and call the buyers and explain what I had found. He claimed he had no idea the horse had ever had any lameness or episodes of laminitis. So I told the buyers exactly what I saw on the films. I also let them know the horse was not lame when I took the pictures.

After supper, the phone rang. It was the client, insanely upset that I took x-rays of the coffin bones instead of the navicular bone. I told him I *always* take several views of the entire foot to get a better view of the navicular bone and the alignment of all the bones so I'm not missing a key piece of information. He was angry because I told the clients about the sinking coffin bones, even though I explained that his son told me to make the phone call. I endured several minutes of profanity and spouting off, letting him vent before setting him straight. My stomach was in knots and my fingers were shaking as I held the phone.

"I understand your frustration, Mr. White. While it's unfortunate to find a problem other than what you were trying to rule-out, I will not lie to my clients. Since your son asked me to give your buyers the results, I gave them an honest assessment of the feet. I did try calling you several times before I discussed anything with your son or your buyers. If I have upset you, I'm very sorry."

There was an awkward silence. After several seconds, my client sheepishly apologized for going off on me. He was angry at his son and himself for the miscommunication. Even though his apology was welcome, my nerves were frazzled beyond belief. I hung up the phone, vowing never to set foot onto his farm again.

That evening Fred came home in a less than desirable mood, so I slipped out to the barn to love on the horses. They had such unique ways of making me feel wonderful despite the day I'd had. I stepped into Ibn's stall. As I caressed the area under his mane, he moved forward and laid his handsome head on my left shoulder as if to offer a big hug. I wrapped my arms around his neck, feeling myself start to relax. Next, I visited Ty's stall. Still being a bit on the shy side, he sidled up next to me, standing very still while I stroked his silky mane and neck. Being in his modest presence made me aware that I'd need to let my tension and stress go before he could feel completely comfortable. I took some deep breaths, letting them out slowly and calmly. Ty's eyes softened and he let out a sigh as we both released our rigidity. I moved onto Stormy's stall. Just like when I first met this precious soul, he gazed intently at me with his soft brown eyes. I stepped closely to him and scratched his shoulders and back. Just being in his presence was peaceful and full of love.

The first winter at the acreage was tough. Blinding snowstorms, big drifts, and melting–freezing patterns hampered efforts to open the sliding doors where my mobile veterinary clinic was parked. I spent many hours shoveling heavy snow just to have the drifts reform. House-call appointments had to be cancelled because I couldn't get the mobile unit out, putting a slight strain on our cash flow. I began to question the decision to move to the country. But those thoughts were quickly dispelled as I observed how happy and healthy the three horses were.

Spring finally arrived. Three horses that were boarding at our acreage for the fall and winter months went home, so Ty, Ibn, and Stormy had the farm to themselves for the time being. My marriage had eroded to a point where the two of us avoided each other whenever possible, at least on my end. Fred didn't seem to comprehend the profound deterioration in our relationship, and still expected intimacy and affection, despite my emotional withdrawal from him. I was miserable.

Late one humid May afternoon, I was sweeping the barn aisle when the weather radio alarm went off. Startled, I dropped the broom on the floor and ran to turn up the volume. There had been a chance of severe weather for northeast Iowa, and I was concerned.

"This is the National Weather Service. A severe storm warning is in effect immediately for northern Grundy and southeastern Butler counties in northeast Iowa.:.," the computer-generated voice continued, "...impacting the towns of Wellsburg, Grundy Center, Dike and New Hartford. The storms are traveling at 50 mph and are capable of damaging winds, large hail, and torrential rain. A tornado cannot be ruled out. Take cover immediately..." I ran to the west doors and saw the ominous cumulonimbus clouds that were billowing up to the southwest. This is *not* good, I concluded. *Got to get the horses inside*—now.

The three boys were in the northern part of the pasture, grazing contentedly. I called their names but they all ignored me, intent on grazing. I quickly grabbed halters and lead ropes and ran down the grassy slope toward them. Seemingly out of nowhere, little blasts of cold intertwined with the hot, humid air, a telltale sign the storm was approaching rapidly. The horses suddenly became uneasy, and I could see the whites of each one's eyes. As if someone had pulled the trigger on a gun to signal the start of a race, the trio exploded into a frenzied gallop to the barn. I sprinted back up the hill, dragging lead ropes through the grass and dirt, frantic to get to the barn before the fury of the storm hit. Just as I reached the barn, tentacles of lightning spread across the entire sky, eerily illuminating the ominous clouds. The horses ran to their respective stalls, so I only had to shut their doors.

The wind fiercely pushed against the sliding doors at the west end of the barn as I struggled hard to close them. The bottom of the door had to fit inside the metal tracks to prevent the wind from ripping it away from the top hangers. The harder I shoved, the stronger the wind blew against the doors. *"Damn it!"* I yelled, *"Help me out!"* as if summoning some supernatural help. Fighting back tears of fear, frustration, and failure, I momentarily succumbed to the wind. I was tired of struggling to make things work that weren't going to work, like my marriage. Tired of struggling to stay positive. Tired of pretending that everything was okay. Tired of life in general. I leaned into the steel door, head in my hands, and shed tears of self-pity while the wind shrieked loudly around the door frame.

Supernatural "spirits" must have been listening, because the wind subsided for a few seconds and the door slid into the track. I heaved it shut and snapped the side latches into place. Before I had time to run to the house, the weather radio's alarm sounded again. The audio blurted, "Tornado warning for southeastern Butler County until 4:30 p.m. Radar indicates a severe thunderstorm with rotation located approximately… affecting the towns of …and New Hartford". I felt goosebumps forming on my arms. I'd only been in a tornado once, as a child, and remembered how the basement windows popped out in front of me as our parents made us kids huddle under a heavy table in the family room.

My immediate concern was for the horses. Four years before we bought the acreage, a weak tornado had demolished the original barn, hurling it into the field across the gravel road. Fortunately, all of the horses were gone to a show when the twister hit. Now we were inside the rebuilt barn, in exactly the same spot as the original. Would a tornado strike the same area *twice?*

I felt a strong urge to remain in the barn with my boys, even though it was a death trap if a tornado hit. I couldn't imagine going on with life if something happened to the horses. *God*, I silently prayed, *please spare the horses from harm. But if you take them, you have to take me too.* I felt confident that God knew my intentions and my pain. Whatever happened, we would all be in Perfect Hands.

I pulled a beer out of the refrigerator in the barn and sat down in a lounge chair between Ty and Ibn's stall. Drawing an icy sip from the can, I felt oddly at peace as mad gusts of wind and small debris hammered the west doors of the barn. Even the horses remained calm, quietly munching on leftover hay as the storm bore down.

For several minutes, wind blew relentlessly. Lights flickered and soon the power went off. I sat in the dark, sipping on my beer, reflecting on how the horses came into my life and how they had been my rock. Hail began to pelt the metal roof as the sides of the barn shuddered and shook in response to the ferocious wind gusts. *Please God, spare the horses if this barn goes…*

As suddenly as it began, the wind stopped. Raindrops tapped against the metal roof of the barn as the storm proceeded eastward. Amazingly, there was no damage to the acreage except for small branches that were scattered across the yard. A brilliant rainbow adorned the eastern sky as the clouds parted and the sun reappeared. As the horses galloped back outside to graze for a few more hours, I felt enormous gratitude for their safety.

In 2008, four years after I moved from the acreage, a deadly EF-5 tornado slammed into it, ripping every building, tree, and piece of equipment into shreds. Twelve people, and an unknown number of livestock and horses were mercilessly killed by the monstrous storm as it pounded across eastern Iowa. All five horses that had been stabled at the acreage at the time died; the bodies of two were never found.

Chapter 8
Upheaval

I was spending as much time away from home as possible to avoid confrontations with Fred. The mobile veterinary business was doing well, although gas prices had risen to almost $4.00 per gallon, cutting into the profit margins considerably. Fuel prices were expected to continue rising and the mobile clinic only averaged six miles to the gallon in good weather. Disheartened by the pressure from my husband to find somewhere else to work and the bleak economic market, I sold the mobile clinic and accepted a position as an associate veterinarian in a busy small animal practice twenty miles away.

Carrie was now in her second semester of her senior year in high school and was well aware of the situation between her dad and me. One evening before Fred came home, Carrie cornered me in the kitchen. With contempt in her voice, she said, "Mom. You are *not* happy with Dad. Why are you staying with him?" The question caught me off guard.

"Carrie," I sighed wearily, gathering my thoughts. "You graduate in a few months. This is supposed to be your best year of high school. You need to focus on your school work and having fun with your friends. Where did you get the idea that your dad and I should split up?"

"Mom," she retorted, "I *don't* like the way Dad acts toward you. Don't you think it's hard on *me*, listening to you two fight all the time? I hear a lot more than you think, especially when he's being sarcastic. You always told me to never put up with that kind of stuff myself, yet *you* do!" She stomped away in disgust.

Carrie was absolutely right. I openly criticized other women for staying with men that were emotionally, verbally and/or physically abusive to their women, but here I was, paralyzed in a relationship that wasn't going to be resolved. On several occasions, Fred accused me of loving the horses more than him. It was sadly true. The horses accepted *me* unconditionally. They didn't care how much money I made, what I wore, or what my hobbies were. They just loved me for *me*.

For five years, I had been in family counseling with Kent, a Christian advisor, who had considerable experience with relationship challenges. Fred attended a few of the sessions, then felt it was a waste of time and money. He never went back. I'm not sure if he didn't think it was his responsibility to make some minor changes that could positively impact our relationship or if he just didn't care. Most of the time, I was the one at fault.

During one particularly difficult session where Kent was probing deeply, attempting to get me to *really* acknowledge the condition of our marriage, he asked a question that I could not begin to fathom. "What do you see the two of you doing together once Carrie is out of the house? How will you spend your free time together, Barbara?" Kent prodded.

The question caused a moment of intense anxiety for me. *Free time with him? We go our separate ways now! There's really nothing I want to do together! Why subject myself to more anguish than I'm already going through?*

Kent sensed my tension and pushed on. "What about vacations? Where will you two go and what will you be doing? How will you spend your weekends together?"

I sat quietly, desperately searching for any hint of pleasure I could envision between the two of us if we went out for an evening or away for a weekend. I thought about my friends; some went on cruises, others went to music concerts and games. Fred was a homebody and rarely liked to go away unless it was watch a ball game and drink with one of his friends.

After several moments, I turned to my counselor and informed him, "I can't answer your questions. I just can't see us together doing 'fun' things. It kind of makes me feel strange just thinking about it."

"Well, then I think you should separate from him."

I was shocked to hear my marriage consultant speak those words. I thought counselors were trained to help people save their marriages, not dissolve them. Besides, as a Christian counselor, Kent would never encourage a person to leave, or so I thought.

"God hates divorce." I sank down into the plush arm chair and tried to hide the tears that were forming.

Kent leaned forward in his chair, looked me directly in the eye, and gently asked, "Do you really think God wants you to be miserable?"

"No," I whispered, "not the God I know."

"I don't believe He does either," Kent agreed. "You've done your part in trying to make this relationship work; now it's up to you to decide to move on or not."

I nodded weakly. "I know you're right, but I still feel like a failure for not getting this to work. We'll have been married twenty years this May. What could I have done to prevent this, Kent? I feel like I've given it all I have. There's *nothing* left," I murmured, sinking further into the chair.

Kent removed his glasses and rubbed his eyes. Leaning back in his chair with his hands crossed behind his head, he sighed deeply. He looked intently at me without saying a word for what seemed like an eternity. "Have you thought about how you would end it." It was more of a statement than a question.

"You mean the marriage?"

"No. Your life."

I gasped at Kent's question. Though I never had a conscious thought about suicide, Kent sensed that I was extremely unhappy and suffered from situational depression.

"I don't have any idea why you asked me that." My face reddened in embarrassment at Kent's question. "Of course I've never thought of 'ending it.'"

"You're a veterinarian. You have access to some pretty powerful drugs. Again, have you thought about how you might end your life?"

I suddenly felt lightheaded and out of breath. Kent knew intuitively what my subconscious thoughts had been. At one time, during a really "dark" day, I wondered if life got unbearable enough, could I actually inject some euthanasia solution into my arm? On the day of the tornado warning, I was prepared to die with the horses if the storm took their lives. His perception had been right.

"Kent, I could never, ever do that. I love my daughter and my animals too much. There might have been a time when those thoughts briefly visited me, but no—absolutely not—I won't do that."

"Well, good, Barbara, I wanted to hear that. Think strongly about what we discussed today. See you next Tuesday."

That evening, I analyzed what Kent had said. I prayed to God, asking for grace to leave the marriage. What happened next shocked me. As I began to drift off to sleep in my bedroom, a "movie" flooded my mind. It was a fast-forward version of all of the events and dialogue that brought me to seek *permission* to end my dysfunctional relationship. In a very short period of time, the negative episodes during the marriage flashed before me, as if they were happening *now*. I had forgotten just how disturbing some of them had been—things I couldn't tell *anyone*. *That* was my sign from God that I needed to get out.

The next day, I secured an apartment in town. My goal was to get everything arranged before I told Fred I was moving out. When I got the courage to tell him, he took the news oddly well. My biggest concern was for the horses and where I could keep them until I found a permanent home for them. Fred didn't want anything to do with the horses, but offered to let me keep them on the acreage temporarily. I arranged for a neighbor girl to take care of the boys in the morning, then I would do the evening chores while Fred was working out. I thought the less we ran into each other, the better.

Two weeks later, I filed for divorce. Fred's attitude turned completely around, apparently thinking I had cried wolf and would come to my senses. First, the phone calls started, begging me to reconsider and telling me I couldn't live without him. Then I would catch him driving by my apartment at various times of the evening. I felt it would be wise to move the horses as soon as possible, given the eerie feeling I had. I nervously dialed Karen's number. She answered on the first ring.

Karen was happily remarried and living on a beautiful, secluded acreage with a nice setup for horses about a half an hour away. She listened carefully as I explained why I was anxious to move the horses. Bless her heart, I could keep the horses at her place, where each horse would have their own stall along with three acres of pasture. All I had to provide was feed and bedding. We planned to move them two evenings later while Fred was still at the YMCA.

I drove back out to our acreage to feed the horses that evening.

Upon opening the barn door, the smell of gasoline was so strong it created an instant headache. I found it hard to breathe and my eyes teared up from the intense fumes. I felt goose bumps forming on my arms. *Where is that smell coming from? And* why *are there gasoline fumes in here?* Covering my nose and mouth with a rag, I reached for the light switch. *Oh no, the horses were already in! Fred must have brought the horses in early—but why?* My heart was pounding from fear and panic. I ran down the aisle and opened all of the doors, letting fresh breezes replace the toxic fumes. My immediate thought was, *Is he planning to burn the barn down?* That happened to a woman earlier in the year, not too far away from where we lived. Twenty high-dollar quarter horses perished in a fire rumored to have had a suspicious cause. Even though the fire was most likely due to a faulty electrical heater, I couldn't get the thought of arson of my mind.

Anger quickly took over any fear I experienced—gut-wrenching, heart-pounding fury. No way was I going to let my precious horses stay in this barn one more night! My fingers were shaking so badly I could barely hit the right buttons on the cell phone to call Karen back.

"Oh my God, Barb, I'll be right over to get them. Grab their feed and tack and anything else you need to get out of there tonight!" I sensed the urgency in her voice. Karen was a volunteer firefighter and emergency responder. Not much intimidated her. She could handle the situation if Fred came home early.

Luckily, the horses loaded quickly and without incident. I grabbed feed, halters, and all the tack I could load in Karen's pickup. The rest would have to wait. We were running out of time to get away from the property and into the privacy of Karen's acreage.

Chapter 9
Transitions

Ty, Ibn, and Stormy settled in well at Karen's acreage. Each had access to the three acre pasture and spacious stalls that were deep with pine shavings. Access to Karen's acreage was private; there was a wooded lane from the county blacktop road to the house. The horses liked to graze toward the north end of the pasture, furthest from the barn. When Ibn would spot me driving up the lane in my red pickup, he would burst into a full gallop. His comical little frenzy caused Ty and Stormy to join him in the race to the barn. They knew their supper would soon be served.

I helped Karen with chores to help offset the costs of keeping the horses at her place. Cleaning stalls was therapy for me—I didn't have to think. It was good physical exercise, and I compared flinging the poop onto the manure pile to getting rid of the "crap" in my life.

Karen and I rekindled our friendship through mutual challenges. Karen had felt emotionally abandoned during the last several years of her marriage, and she eventually left her husband, relinquishing her share of their farm. Oftentimes, after getting chores done, the two of us cracked open a bottle of white zinfandel and reminisced about our trials and tribulations throughout our relationships. At one time in our lives, we couldn't imagine laughing at our situations. Now, either the wine or the absurdity of the issues we recalled initiated bouts of uncontrolled giggling.

"I remember when Black Dog was barking incessantly one night," I told Karen. Black Dog was a black lab that actually belonged to the people we bought our acreage from, but he didn't like his new place and traveled several miles across country to return to his "home."

Black Dog's former owners finally gave up trying to keep him at their place and let us adopt him.

"So Carrie and I were downstairs talking in the family room. Fred had already gone to bed. All of a sudden, he yells at us to *make* Black Dog stop barking." I shook my head, recalling that the easiest solution would be to just close the bedroom window.

"You can't make him stop barking," I said. "He probably has a coon cornered."

Black Dog's bark was more of a muffled "woof" sound instead of a harsh bark. "Apparently Fred didn't want to shut the window, so he comes charging down the stairs, glaring at me and Carrie. He didn't say anything, but I could tell he definitely was not amused. He throws his hiking boots on without lacing them up, heads out the basement door, and jogs in his underwear and loose boots across the gravel road to where the dog had cornered something. It was dark enough we couldn't see exactly where he ended up."

Karen must have gotten a visual of the scene because she started to snicker. "Carrie and I were looking at each other like 'what the heck.' We could hear him yelling at the dog to shut up but the 'woof-woofing' kept going on and on." I demonstrated the "woof" by lowering my voice and stretching my neck up high, like a dog does when it's intent on barking. Karen busted out laughing, spewing drops of wine all over her white T-shirt. Her contagious laugh caused me to join in, and for the next few minutes we laughed so hard we couldn't catch our breath.

During the next few months, I started to feel vibrant and alive again. Spending time with the horses and knowing they were safe from harm eased my tension immensely. Although I yearned to have the acreage back, my income could not support any updating, increase in taxes, or unexpected emergencies that could crop up. Instead of mourning my perceived losses, I rekindled old friendships and sprouted new ones.

Through careful planning by some good friends, I met Gary at Bear Creek trout stream on an unusually warm afternoon in late February. My friends, Bob and Chris, were trying to play matchmaker but the mere thought of dating after twenty years of marriage frightened me. Although I yearned to have male friends, I was adamant about not getting into a serious relationship. However, Bob and Chris, who had both gone through recent divorces, insisted that the four of us just meet up as friends—no strings attached. I insisted on driving separately; that way, if the meeting didn't go well for me, I could leave at will.

That afternoon was the turning point in my new life. Gary admitted his love for horses, the outdoors, fishing; he was a country boy at heart. Furthermore, he was interested and engaged in what I had to say. He proved to be the perfect gentleman, carrying my fishing tackle and opening car doors. Over the next few weeks, we developed a solid relationship, talking for hours until our cell phone batteries died. When Gary was back in town from being on the road, our "date nights" were often spent cleaning stalls, sipping beer on Karen's deck, and hanging out with the horses.

"I never dreamed I'd enjoy pitching manure," Gary laughed as he swung a forkful of road apples onto the manure pile. "I hated doing this on the dairy farm, but every minute I spend with you is a good one, no matter what we're doing."

"Ha! I feel the same way, Gary. You know, it never seems to matter what we're doing. I just love the fact we can be together. After all, I've waited all my life for you," I said, smiling. "Hey, I really appreciate the help. Thanks for 'pitching in,' no pun intended!"

"My pleasure, ma'am." He grinned mischievously as he scooped up a pile of wet shavings and pretended to toss it at me.

Although the horses accepted Gary's presence, Stormy was hesitant to let him near his face and ears. The old emotional traumas surfaced as Stormy winced and pulled his head back repeatedly. "Hey, boy, nobody's going to ever hurt you again," Gary said softly as he stroked the bay gelding's neck. "You're safe, buddy. No reason to be afraid of me." Stormy sighed, and turned his head toward Gary as if to say, "I know, I just need time." Once Gary learned of Stormy's former abuse, he spent extra time petting and grooming him. Within a short period of time, Stormy completely trusted the man who assured him no more harm would come his way.

Six weeks after we met, Gary and I were married in a simple ceremony in a small church situated alongside the Volga River. Never in my wildest dreams would I have imagined marrying after knowing one another for a mere six weeks. But we knew that when God closes a door, another one opens…

Chapter 10
Settling In

Shortly after we were married, we brought the horses to our own rented acreage in northeast Iowa. The property was on top of a hill, bordered on three sides by thick timber and hills. The gravel road leading from the county blacktop to our house was steep and curvy, with a high limestone bank on one side and a sharp drop to the valley on the other. A gigantic field bordered by timber was located directly east from the house. Every evening, several herds of deer came out to graze, providing endless entertainment for the horses.

The boys had an empty corncrib that served as a walk-in shelter from their pasture. In the summer, it allowed good air flow from the slats in the sideboards and the open door to the south. In the wintertime, the north door could be pulled shut to block the wind. Plastic sheeting on the sides kept the wind from blowing through the building.

The timber directly to the west of the property was heavily wooded and extremely hilly. There were several all-terrain vehicle and tractor trails that led from the barnyard to the valley floor below. Several springs and streams traversed through the ravine, creating challenging water crossings. I had lots of fun riding Stormy through the timber, although it took some time to acclimate him to the "scary stuff" in the woods, like invisible deer, turkeys, and even shadows.

Since Ibn's feet were becoming increasingly tender, Stormy became my main riding horse. Ty was approaching twenty-three years of age, and although he was still quite rideable, I didn't want to stress his aging joints on the rigorous trails. He was also Ibn's "babysitter," as Ibn hated being alone. He would run frantically if left behind, which played havoc on his feet for several days afterward.

We relished our time with the three horses. Many summer evenings were spent brushing, stroking, and just hanging out with the boys. It was sad to think of how fast time was slipping by, and that Ty and Ibn were showing their age. Long gone were the days of horse shows, dressage clinics, and organized trail rides. I vowed to make their last years as pleasant as possible, offering them deep bedding in the wintertime, fans in the summertime, the best foot care year 'round, plenty of quality hay, and lots of love and hugs.

And of course, an endless supply of carrots for Ibn.

Chapter 11
Saying Goodbye

I awakened to a beautiful clear-blue-sky day in early June. Early morning songbirds chirped and caroled harmoniously. A soft breeze swept across the room as I stretched and rolled out of bed. *It's going to be a fantastic day, I thought,* reaching for my robe. *I've got the morning off, no errands to run; maybe I'll get some rock hunting or hiking in this morning. God knows I need some time to myself after the work week I've had.*

As I headed down the steps, a nagging feeling hit me. The night before, Ibn had acted strangely, not particularly interested in his food. Gary had commented he didn't think Ibn looked well. I attributed his "off" behavior to the pergolide he had been given him to control his Cushing's disease. It was a difficult balance between controlling the illness with the drug and dealing with side effects from the medication.

Concerned, I threw on my chore clothes and headed out to check on the horses. The uneasiness intensified as I walked quickly toward the corncrib. None of the horses were grazing in the pasture around their shelter, which was unusual. Normally, all three boys would be enjoying the early morning grass before the mid-day sun made it uncomfortable to be out.

"Hey boys!" I called as I approached their shelter. None of the horses whinnied back. Puzzled, I picked up the pace. As I rounded the corner of the corncrib, I gasped. Ibn was down on his side, laying directly in the entryway of their shelter, trapping Ty and Stormy inside. A wave of anxiety and dread washed over me. *Oh my God, is he dead? Ibn, please, buddy, please be okay!*

As I knelt down beside him, Ibn slowly raised his head. "Oh Ibn, what is going on?" I pleaded. "Help me out, big guy; let's get up!"

Groaning in pain, Ibn slowly rolled himself onto his belly and rested his chin on the ground. His breathing was labored, with nostrils flaring at every attempt to inhale. His beautiful brown eyes were glazed over and he made no attempt to make eye contact with me. The look of surrender was written all over his body. The once proud and expressive horse was giving up.

Ibn's demeanor told me what needed to be done. Confirmation came to me as I felt the bounding arterial pulses above the hooves. Ibn's feet were hot to the touch; one foot was draining from an abscess. Trying to push my own despair and dread aside, I stroked his neck and assured him that he would not suffer anymore. This would be his final episode of laminitis, the last chapter of his life on earth.

I sat beside my friend and told him what I had to do. Suffering relentless pain was not part of the plan. Living without quality of life was not part of the plan. Assisting his transition into the afterlife *would be* part of the plan. I encouraged Ty and Stormy to gather with me to offer our final good-byes. Both horses were unusually quiet, as if *they knew*. Stormy stepped forward and gently nudged his friend with his nose, encouraging him to get up. Ibn started to turn his head toward Stormy, then let it drop back to the ground, groaning as the pain persisted. Ty chose to remain in the background, seemingly unsure what he should do.

One of the most difficult things veterinarians have to do is to euthanize an animal. Veterinarians are trained to "fix" an animal, not to end its life. I had rehearsed this scenario in my head many times, as I was convinced it would be best to have someone Ibn knew and trusted administering the final injection. But now I was sitting on the "other" side of the fence, the side of the animal owner having to make the dreaded decision. How I empathized with pet owners in this scenario! *Oh God, help me through this,* I prayed silently. *Give me the strength and the guidance to help this poor horse end his suffering and enter the Light.* Tears flowed freely down my face as I called upon Divine help. Moments later, I was able to detach from the situation emotionally as I had trained myself to do when euthanizing clients' animals. I picked myself up off the ground, slowly walked to the house, and prepared the drugs needed for the procedure.

After administering a heavy sedative that would also alleviate a good majority of Ibn's pain, I inserted an intravenous catheter. Then I asked Ibn to help me. He would have to get up and walk a few feet away from the entrance of the corncrib. Once the sedative began to set in, I slipped a halter around Ibn's head and tugged gently on the lead rope. At first, Ibn didn't respond. Yet he had to get up before the full effect of the sedative kicked in. I tugged the lead rope a bit more firmly. Ibn grunted, rolled the rest of the way onto his belly, then with one heroic effort, lunged to his feet. He swayed slightly from the effects of the injection as we walked the short distance to the corner of the pasture.

I petted Ibn's neck and whispered, "I love you, my friend. See you on the other side." Then I slipped the syringe into the catheter and slowly injected the lethal solution as I had done so many times during my career. Hot tears stung my eyes as I pushed the plunger of the syringe. Before I injected barely half of the solution, our enchanting white horse peacefully slipped to the ground and took his last breath.

Through the experience of euthanizing animals, I had always felt that when an animal went down quietly and peacefully, they were more than ready for passage into the next realm. Many dogs willingly offered their leg for the injection to be given, as if to say, "Please help me end this suffering. I can't do it anymore."

I placed the stethoscope gently on Ibn's chest and listened for any signs of a heartbeat. There was nothing. Death was confirmed. I sat beside the lifeless body with knees drawn toward my chest and started to sob. The finality of the situation punched me hard. There is no turning back; no bringing that wonderful creature back to life. Not that I would wish him back. I wouldn't want him to suffer. *It just hurts so much!* Watching an animal take its last breath or listening to its heartbeat fade away until deathly silence is complete finality. There is a sense of loss that only those who have experienced it can understand.

Ty and Stormy were still standing in the entryway to the corncrib. I gathered my supplies and moved away from Ibn to give his buddies an opportunity to acknowledge their friend's passing. Ty was the first to approach. He hesitantly walked toward the body, then stopped and snorted. He inched forward with his nose to the ground. Once he reached his best friend, he drew in a deep breath and nuzzled the back of the white horse's neck. Ty abruptly backed up, almost colliding with Stormy. The two horses broke into a trot, circling Ibn's body several times before stopping to sniff their friend for the last time. Then they sauntered out to the pasture to graze. Closure for the remaining two boys was now complete.

Chapter 12
The Unthinkable

The following morning, our neighbor, Steve, arrived bright and early to dig the grave. Gary took a few hours off work to help with the process, assisting with opening and closing gates and keeping the other two horses occupied. Gary insisted that I remain inside the house, as he didn't want me subjected to the sight of Ibn's body being loaded into the bucket of the backhoe. Although I was concerned for Ty and Stormy, Gary promised to keep an eye on the boys and give them a few flakes of hay while Steve did his job.

"Hey, hon," Gary said softly as he was leaving the house, "I picked out a place at the edge of the field, just inside the timber. It's right along the ridge overlooking the spring." I knew exactly where Gary was referring to. It was a beautiful setting, with abundant wildflowers and exceptional views of the forest valley.

"Thanks, Gary, that will be such a nice resting place. I appreciate you taking time off work to help out. I don't think I can handle it all right now." I pushed a tear back from the corner of my eye.

"That's why I'm here, babe. I'm your husband, remember? I want to be here for you." Gary stepped back inside the kitchen and gave me a big hug.

"I know, it's just that—" my voice trailed off as I caught myself making comparisons. It didn't matter now. I had Gary's complete love and support. "Thank you for being *you,*" I whispered. "I don't know what I'd do without you."

Gary kissed me on the cheek, grabbed his cap, and continued out the door. "You stay here until I come back and let you know when everything's done."

Ty and Stormy quietly munched on hay while Gary and Steve prepared the grave. Occasionally, Ty stopped chewing and turned to look toward the corner of the pasture where his friend's body had been.

"You would have been pleased to see how gently Steve handled Ibn's body," Gary told me. "He handled him like it was his own animal." Reaching into a pocket on his jacket, he said, "Here, I saved something for you," and pulled out a lock of Ibn's silvery tail hair. He had thoughtfully clipped it before Ibn was laid in his grave. I fingered the thick strands of his tail as another tear rolled down my cheek. "Thank you," I murmured, grateful for the physical memoir.

Gary left for work soon afterward. He was already behind schedule, which meant there was a good possibility he would have to stay out overnight. Fertilizer had to be hauled no matter what. I was filling in for another veterinary clinic in the afternoon, so I had a few hours to myself. The yard needed mowing, and I thought it would be a good distraction until I had to leave. As I backed the riding lawn mower out of the machine shed, I noticed Ty sniffing at the ground where Ibn had been put to sleep. *That's pretty normal; he's just like any other animal inhaling the scent of another*, I surmised. Stormy had his head buried in the last flake of hay Gary had put out at the far end of the lot, not particularly interested in anything except eating.

After several passes through the front lawn with the mower, something caught my eye. Ty was down, rolling in the dirt where Ibn's body had laid overnight. I stopped the mower and watched as he rolled slowly from side to side. He rolled onto his chest in an upright position, tucked his legs under him, and rose to his feet. Most horses shake themselves off after rolling, especially if they roll in dirt and dust, but Ty did not. This was unusual for him. I continued to observe him, making sure he was okay before I started the mower back up. I had heard of animals, especially dogs, rolling to get the scent of a beloved friend in their fur, but hadn't witnessed it until now. *My poor Ty, oh I feel so badly for you*, I mouthed silently. *I know this is hard for you buddy. I feel your pain. Oh, how I wish I could make it okay with you.*

I started the mower back up and made another pass around the front yard. As I rounded the corner of the house, I again saw Ty's legs buckle *in exactly the same spot*. I shut the mower off and watched. His

65

body made a dull thud as he dropped onto the dirt. This time, he rolled violently. Instead of getting up, he lay on his side for an unusually long time, then he rolled onto his back, with all four of his legs pointing upward.

My stomach tightened, as I knew that when a horse is on its back with its legs in the air, it is not a good sign. That type of posture almost always indicates a severe episode of colic (intestinal pain). Colic can be mild or life-threatening, depending on what is causing the pain.

Greatly concerned by Ty's odd behavior, I jumped off the mower and ran to grab my stethoscope and emergency bag. When I reached him, Ty was standing up, but his breathing was labored and the sides of his abdomen appeared taut and sunken in. When a veterinarian listens for "gut sounds" in a horse, there are four quadrants to check: upper left, lower left, upper right, lower right. Gurgles and bubbling noises are normal; silence is not. A quiet gut means nothing is moving. Each quadrant relates anatomically to a specific portion of the intestinal tract, so sound or silence in each quadrant helps the doctor localize the problem.

Ty had *no* gut sounds at all. I picked up his lip to check his mucous membrane color. It was unusually pale. Healthy horses have visibly pink gums. I was quite concerned, as Ty had never been sick one day in his twenty-five years of life. I hurriedly drew up a syringe full of a pain reliever and anti-inflammatory drug, then slowly injected it into Ty's jugular vein. The drug usually took ten to fifteen minutes to work, if it *was* going to be therapeutic. I looped a lead rope around Ty's neck and walked him slowly to help his intestines move.

Despite the injection and walking, Ty's intestinal tract didn't respond. After fifteen minutes, there was alarming silence in the stethoscope as I checked both sides of his abdomen. I drew up another syringe of the anti-inflammatory and pain medication and injected again. Concern for the elderly equine was accelerating. The great majority of horses with a simple "gas" colic respond within minutes to the medication. Those who didn't were usually suffering from something more serious than trapped gas in the colon. I checked my watch impatiently as another ten minutes ticked away. Nervously, I placed the bell of the stethoscope over Ty's upper left quadrant, then the lower left…there was no hint of movement in the intestinal tract.

Panic set in as I listened for *any* hint that the gut had started to respond. I knew that the probability of something more complicated affecting Ty's gastrointestinal tract was very real. Throughout the four years that I served as a volunteer on ISU's veterinary college Colic Watch Team, many of the horses that were referred to the veterinary hospital with severe colic either collapsed and died in the trailer, or didn't survive surgery to repair a twist or obstruction in the gut. I shuddered as I recalled a few of the dreadful cases I had dealt with, either while on the colic watch team or in my own veterinary practice. Horses' digestive tracts are very sensitive to changes, whether the changes are related to stress, diet, parasites, toxins, and other factors. Colic is the number one killer of horses of all ages. I *had* to keep trying to alleviate Ty's abdominal discomfort and dysfunction. All I had in my "toolbox" was pain and anti-inflammatory drugs. Had the scenario been fast-forwarded ten years, I would have used medical-grade essential oils, acupressure, and energy medicine to help work my precious geldings through their issues.

A third injection into Ty's jugular vein finally began working. Faint gurgles and swishing noises were music to my ears as I assessed his gut again. Though the motility was weak, it was there. "Thank God," I sighed, finally. "Now please, Ty, show me some signs you're feeling better. How about nibbling on some hay, or passing a nice pile of poop?" I could breathe a huge sigh of relief if Ty passed manure. Horses with a twisted intestine rarely passed manure or had any kind of appetite.

After a few moments, Ty ambled over to the dwindling flake of hay Stormy had been eating. Ty sniffed what remained, and picked out a few stalks of alfalfa, chewing slowly at first. He ended up eating the rest of the flake, then walked a few yards away and passed a nice pile of normal-appearing manure. I was ecstatic at the reversal in his health. The next time I listened to his abdomen, Ty had good gut sounds in all four areas. *Finally*, I thought, it's over. *My boy is going to be fine. Wow, let's not have any more excitement for a while, though, Mr. Tysheyn!*

I threw a few more flakes of hay for Stormy and Ty to work on, checked their water tank, then prepared to leave for the Readlyn Veterinary Clinic. One last checkup on Ty before I left turned out normal; Ty's gum color was pink again, heart rate and respirations were back to normal, and he had good gut sounds. What set the colic episode into motion, I reasoned, was the stress from Ibn's passing. There had been no other changes in their feeding routine, grazing, or overall husbandry. It tugged at my heart to realize how tight the bond between Ty and Ibn had been. He truly grieved for his favorite companion. Hopefully Stormy would help fill the void for Ty.

There was something that still bothered me as I started the hour-long drive to the clinic, but I couldn't pinpoint exactly what it was. Ty had been with me for nineteen years and I knew him like the back of my hand. When I told Jen, my good friend and veterinary assistant at the clinic about the morning's events, she offered to keep the schedule light.

"We're not real busy between six and seven tonight. If you want to cut out a little early, I'll make sure the schedule stays open," Jen offered.

"Thanks Jen, but he was doing just fine when I left. I don't think I need to leave early."

"Now wait a minute, you just said you felt *something wasn't right*. You *have* to listen to your gut. You're always telling *me* that!" Jen gently scolded.

"Yes, you're right. If we don't have any appointments later, I just might take you up on that. Gary won't be home until late tonight so I should get home and check on the boys before it gets dark," I rationalized.

As I began her drive home, the nagging feeling that something was wrong intensified. It was close to 8:00 p.m. as I turned in our driveway. Neither of the horses were in the pasture, which was unusual since they loved to graze in the early evening after the flies settled down. *Hopefully I didn't leave a gate open,* I contemplated. *Who knows, after the stress of the morning, where my mind is.* I quickly parked the pickup, turned off the ignition and rushed down to the corncrib. My eyes widened in disbelief and horror as I rounded the corner of the building. There was my precious Ty, lying on his side next to the inside wall of the corncrib. There were multiple cuts and scrapes on his face and head caused by violent thrashing. His abdomen bulged behind his rib cage, and his eyes were sunken in with the look of death.

"No, no, nooo!" I screamed. *"Not you too! Oh my God!"*

I fell to my knees, sobbing uncontrollably, as Ty made no attempt to lift his head or give any sign that he was fighting to stay alive. His gums were cold to the touch and purplish in color, indicative of the body

The Infinite Bond

systems shutting down. I vigorously patted him on the neck and rump, urgently attempting to get him to stand. Ty grunted loudly, then rolled one last time, pinning his legs against the wall.

I felt as if someone had just punched me in the stomach with a ball bat. Here was my beautiful, sweet Ty, reduced to a limp, dying body scrunched up tightly against the side of the corn crib. I had only minutes to get him out of that position, as the pressure on his lungs and heart would be fatal. If I had *any* chance of trying to keep him alive, he had to be moved away from the wall immediately. The complicating factor was that horses who are cast are very dangerous to work around. Usually, it takes at least two people to cautiously slip ropes around the front and rear ankles, then carefully pull the ropes until the horse rolls back away from the wall. Because horses are "flight" animals, meaning they will do anything to get away from a situation where they are trapped, people often get kicked or knocked to the ground when the horse is trying desperately to get its legs back under him.

I grabbed my cell phone.

"Hey, babe, what's up?" Gary asked.

"I need help, I need you here *now!*" I shouted. "Ty is cast and I can't move him myself! He's very sick and I'm afraid I'm losing him!!" The words continued to spill out of my mouth so quickly Gary was utterly confused.

"Slow down, hon," Gary said gently. "Start over so I can understand."

I hurriedly gave Gary a summary of the situation.

"Oh no, I'm so sorry to hear that! Oh babe! The radiator hose on the semi blew a few hours ago. I'm waiting on the tow truck to get here. I can't leave the truck and I'm two hours from home yet. I'm so sorry! Can you call Steve to help you? What about Bob?"

"There's no time Gary! I only have a few minutes. I'll have to try moving him by myself. Gotta go."

"Please call me later and let me know what happens," Gary asked. *"Be careful!"*

I grabbed two soft ropes out of the tack room and slipped them over Ty's left front and left rear legs. I had no idea if I was strong enough to move him at all. Saying a quick prayer, I tugged and pulled with every ounce of strength I had left. Finally, after the third attempt, Ty was

69

far enough away from the side of the wall to where he could get up if he wanted. But the old gelding was dying. His heartbeat was faint and rapid; his gums were now a dark shade of purple. His body temperature was so low it wouldn't even register on the thermometer. In a few minutes, Ty's heart and other organs would stop functioning. He moaned and whined with every breath, making it unbearable for me to witness. I sprinted to the truck, grabbed a syringe and bottle of euthanasia solution, and humanely ended his suffering. In less than thirty-six hours, two lives were gone forever.

For several minutes, I sat on the ground beside Ty's lifeless body, numb and ridden with guilt and "what ifs." *What if I'd just stayed home, could I have averted this horrible ending? What if I'd taken him to a referral hospital, could he have survived surgery? What if I had kept him away from Ibn's body, would he not have gotten sick in the first place?*

As the tears flowed unashamedly, I knew subconsciously that there was nothing that could have been done. For a horse with a colon torsion, surgery has to be performed within one or two hours of onset of clinical signs. We lived over three hours away. And we had sold the horse trailer when the three boys were retired from showing, so I would have had to line up a trailer or have someone haul him. Intestinal surgery on a twenty-five year old horse carries a survival rate of only five percent, and that figure doesn't include complications in the post-surgical period. Perhaps the most important consideration was that *Ty wanted to be with Ibn.* I *knew* that based on my strong gut feelings a few months before Ibn died.

I felt a soft breath on the back of my neck. *Stormy!* I'd forgotten completely about him in the course of events. He had a bewildered look in his eyes. After all, he had just witnessed the deaths of his two best friends. "Oh buddy," I cried, "don't you dare die on me too! I can't handle that!" I threw my arms around Stormy's neck and let the next flood of tears cascade down my face and onto his mane. "I love you so much! I'm so sorry, my beautiful boy!" For several minutes, we remained embraced, sharing each other's grief and shock. Stormy took a deep breath, then sighed heavily. I wiped my eyes with the back of my hand, gathered up the supplies, and prepared to place the large blue tarp over Ty's body.

Chapter 13
The Lone Survivor

The immediate concern for Stormy was to get a companion for him as soon as possible. Bob and Chris offered to bring Harmony, an older mare of theirs, to be Stormy's buddy for as long as we needed her. She arrived early the next morning, before Steve started digging the second gravesite. Gary closed the sliding door of the corncrib that led to the pasture so Stormy and Harmony wouldn't be subjected to seeing Ty's body loaded onto the bucket of the backhoe. Stormy had been through enough emotional trauma, and I prayed that Harmony would be the perfect distraction.

Neither horse seemed particularly concerned with the other. Harmony squealed, like mares sometimes do, when she and Stormy first touched noses. (In a horse's world, sniffing nose-to-nose is like humans shaking hands.) After the initial contact, Harmony walked away, dropped her head, and nibbled on a clump of grass. Stormy followed her, interested in continuing their introduction, but Harmony was only focused on eating. She laid her ears back as her new pasture mate approached, warning him to give her some space. Stormy dejectedly turned and walked away.

Over the next week, the two horses warmed up to each other. Although I was glad to have a companion for my "lone survivor," there was a sense of sadness in him that Harmony couldn't remedy. He *had* to be longing for his old buddies. I thought that perhaps a trail ride at the state park would be a good idea. Harmony was a seasoned trail horse, perfect for Gary. Bob and Chris had quiet, well-trained trail horses they would be riding, so I reasoned that Stormy would be fine with me in the saddle even though he hadn't been anywhere new for quite a while.

Stormy was apprehensive and nervous the entire time we were at the park. He bolted once, nearly unseating me. Then toward the end of the ride, on a sandy stretch of trail, Stormy suddenly laid down, forcing me to leap from the saddle to avoid getting a leg crushed. Next, he refused to cross a tiny stream, even when he could see the other horses readily walking across. When he started pitching and becoming frantic, I dismounted, worried for my safety, and walked him the last half mile back to the day camp area. I was exhausted and disappointed in his behavior. It was oddly *not* his normal demeanor.

Once back, everyone stripped their horses of saddles, blankets, and bridles, and tied the horses to their respective places on the outside of the trailer. I offered Stormy a bucket of water, which he refused, so I left it in front of him, hoping he would take a drink before we left for home. As I was running a brush across his sweaty back, Stormy noticed a dark chestnut Arabian being unloaded from a trailer. He flung his head around and let loose with an ear-splitting whinny. His entire body shook and the whinnying continued. Stormy pawed madly at the ground, all to no avail; the chestnut Arabian paid no attention to him. Stormy became frantic, weaving from side to side, attempting to keep the other horse within sight. One of his front legs caught the edge of the water bucket, spilling the water and splashing it on himself. The clash of the bucket and his hooves coupled with the cold water made him panic. He pulled and thrashed fiercely against the rope with all his might until the snap broke. Stormy toppled over backward, then leaped up and trotted off.

I dashed around the trailer and found Stormy standing between two horse trailers. I approached slowly, talking to him in a soothing voice.

"Hey Storm, settle boy. Stay there fella, everything's alright." I saw his eyes soften as I got closer. I held out my hand, coaxing him to move toward me. Two large-framed men had seen Stormy break away and decided to "help" me round him up. Before I could utter a word, the two men ran from opposite directions toward the bay gelding with outstretched arms. Stormy took one look at the two giants closing in on him and bolted off. Horses and riders scurried out of the way as he stormed through the day camp and across the blacktop road. I lost sight of him as he ran back into the forest on the same trail we'd just come back on.

"Oh damn," I exclaimed, *"Now* what are we going to do?"

Bob said firmly, "Let Gary and me get him. When he gets to that water crossing, chances are he'll stop there. Then we can get a rope on him. You stay here; we'll handle it." The two men jogged off toward the trail as I watched helplessly. There were over thirty miles of trails in the state park. *What if they can't get him? What if he runs into other horses on the trail and causes an accident? What if he takes off through the forest and they can't find him?* My mind was consumed with worry. Chris assured me that with Bob's unusual ability to connect with horses, they'd have Stormy back in no time.

Approximately ten minutes later, Bob and Gary emerged from the trees with a bay Arabian gelding following closely behind. "Where and how did you find him?" I asked, amazed at how calm Stormy appeared.

"He stopped at the stream and froze. I walked right up to him, rubbed his neck, and snapped the rope on his halter."

"That was it?" I quizzed.

"That was it," Bob echoed. "What set him off in the first place? All I heard was the commotion when he was banging against the trailer."

"Someone unloaded a chestnut Arab from their trailer," I explained, "and Stormy must have thought it was Ty. He was SO obsessed with that horse. I have to admit, it did look a lot like Ty. When those two cowboys started running at him, Stormy panicked and took off. If those two yahoos would've just stayed out of it, I would have easily caught him."

"Hon, they were just trying to help," Gary offered. "They didn't know Stormy would take off like that."

"I know, but I tried to wave them off. They just kept on running anyway," I said with disgust in my voice.

"Maybe this wasn't such a good idea after all. It's only been two weeks since Ty and Ibn have been gone," Gary speculated.

"I guess not," I sighed. "I just thought it would be good therapy for Stormy."

Over the next few months, Stormy appeared to age quickly. I performed bloodwork and gave him a comprehensive physical exam, but nothing was out of the ordinary. He was a healthy horse, according to his tests.

Barbara Fox, DVM

However, I felt in my heart that Stormy was emotionally distraught over the loss of his buddies.

Eventually, Harmony returned to the Smiths.' Stormy's next companion was Classi, a middle-aged sorrel quarter horse mare. Classi and Stormy got along exceptionally well. Many warm summer afternoons were spent in the shade of the large pine trees surrounding the north fence of their pasture. Although the two horses were good pals, Stormy continued to age rapidly. Although he was only thirteen in actual age, his behavior and personality resembled a much older horse.

I met a large animal veterinarian, Dr. Merle, at an introductory essential oils class. It was my first exposure to holistic health products, and curiosity got the best of me. Dr. Merle was teaching the basics of how essential oils could be used for physical and emotional wellness. At the end of the class, I explained what I was seeing in my boy and asked if there was anything that might help him. Dr. Merle suggested an emotional release. Giving Dr. Merle that "deer in the headlights" look, I sheepishly asked what an emotional release was.

"An emotional release is something that is done for people, but we've recently started doing them on animals," he explained. "There is a lot of emotional baggage that people, and animals too, carry around. If the emotions are 'released,' the body often becomes healthy again."

"That sounds fascinating, but I have to admit it's a little 'out there,' Merle. Who does it around here and how much does it cost?" I asked.

"Well, we've done them on dogs but have yet to try a session on a horse. If you want your horse to be the first, your only expense would be the cost of the oils."

"Do you really think it would help? I mean, sure, I'd like to try it if there's a chance he would benefit by it," I questioned.

"I would be interested to see how a horse responds to an emotional release. Let me get in touch with the people who've done this and set something up."

Five people experienced with essential oils and energy healing showed up at our place a week later. After a brief summary of what was happening with Stormy and the loss of his two best friends earlier in the year, the practitioners gathered around him and gently stroked and rubbed his neck

74

and shoulders until he was relaxed. Then William, the main facilitator of the session, chose an essential oil blend that was touted to instill courage and confidence. He applied a few drops to Stormy's neck, then allowed him to smell the oil blend from the bottle. The gentle gelding inhaled deeply. Next, William took another bottle from his case, removed the cap, and let Stormy smell it. This time, Stormy yawned widely, which I learned was a sign of releasing. For the next half an hour, various oils were given, either aromatically or topically, depending on Stormy's "preference". If he turned away from an oil, it was not forced on him.

At one point deep into the session, he dropped his nose closely to the ground. Stormy blinked rapidly, making chewing motions with his mouth. At the same time, his facial muscles writhed into strange contortions. One of the healers quietly said, "Oh, poor boy, he's bawling his eyes out." I was amazed; it truly looked like he was sobbing. For five full minutes Stormy continued this behavior while the healers continued to place oils that were calming and soothing on his back.

I was loosely holding the lead rope. I whispered to Merle, "When will you know when he's done releasing these feelings?" William overheard the question and answered, "He'll let us know. Just watch."

After orange essential oil was dropped onto his back, Stormy suddenly jerked the lead rope out of my hand, backed up with lightning speed, spun, and took off galloping across the pasture. He stopped momentarily to roll. He got up, shook himself furiously, then exploded into a full-blown run. After the second pass across the pasture, he halted. *This* time, he looked just like the young and vibrant Stormy I remembered so well. He stood with head and neck majestically high in the air and tail curled up over his back. He blew through his nostrils, making a shrill whistle, then bucked in place and took off galloping.

The healing practitioners were astonished at his beauty and his presence. They had never been around an Arabian horse, so I explained that this was typical Arabian behavior, something this breed has been famous for. Stormy gave an incredible "show," prancing animatedly back to the group of healers and snorting one last time.

I had tears of relief in my eyes as I witnessed the incredible metamorphosis in my beautiful boy. The old Stormy was back! His eyes were full of life and expression again! Oh, how I wished I had known about this therapy sooner. It was so heartwarming to see him happy again! I wasn't sure how to tell Gary what had taken place this afternoon, though. He was due to be home tonight and I had no clue of what to tell him in plain words what an emotional release was, or even what essential oils *were*. I decided to give it some time and see if Stormy continued to thrive after today's events. Then I would ease into the discussion.

Whenever Gary arrived home, the first thing he did was greet Stormy. He always took a few minutes to pet him and give him a handful of oats. This was their bonding time. He and Stormy had developed a relationship of trust and respect. On this particular evening, Gary sensed a difference. He couldn't pinpoint it, but he noticed a spring in Stormy's step, a sharper look in his eye, and a renewed physical appearance.

"Hey hon, I'm home," Gary announced as he dumped his driver's log and lunchbox on the table.

I walked into the kitchen and hugged my husband. "Good to have you home, lover! I've missed you!"

"I missed you too, babe. Hey, what's up with Stormy?" Gary inquired.

"Why do you ask? Is there something wrong?"

"No, but there's something 'different' about him. Like he's younger again. I haven't seen him like that in a long time," Gary noted.

I proceeded to tell him the story of the emotional release session and about how it changed our "lone survivor" so drastically.

"Never in a million years would I have guessed that a few oils could make such a huge difference in our boy," I remarked. "It's unbelievable."

"I know!" Gary exclaimed. "I couldn't believe that was Stormy!"

"I just hope it lasts. I'd just love to see him continue as he is now," I replied.

Stormy continued to thrive mentally and emotionally for the next few years, sharing his pasture with various horses that friends let us "borrow." However, each of the loaned horses eventually had to go home and there were no suitable replacements available. We decided to board Stormy at a riding stable a few miles from our home so he would have constant company. Most of the clients at the stable were trail riders, so almost every Saturday was spent riding with the group through the beautiful timber and streams surrounding the stable.

Stormy shared a large dry lot with a handsome palomino quarter horse gelding named Spud. The two horses hit it off immediately. They were often seen cantering around their lot playing "tag." Spud was quiet and shy around people but when he was with Stormy, his playful personality shined. Spud's owners never came out to see their golden horse, which surprised me.

"Just thought I'd let you know that Spud is going to a sale this weekend," the owner of the stable informed me. "His owners already have two other horses and want to downsize. I'll be putting two of Bill's horses in with Stormy. Since you guys have been riding together so much, there shouldn't be any problems with having to introduce them."

"Oh, thanks for the heads-up." I said as I tried to hide my disappointment. I was concerned about Stormy losing another friend. The *last* thing she wanted to subject him to was another emotional upheaval. "Spud and Stormy get along so well, Mike. Gee, I hate to see him go. What sale is he going to?"

"Some Palomino sale in Minnesota," he replied. "They think they can get more money out of him up there because of his color. Seems like no one around here wanted to offer what they were asking.

"I had no idea he was even for sale," I confided. "May I ask what his price was?"

"They had set his price firmly at eighteen hundred dollars. Seems like a little high for a sixteen-year old horse though."

"Wish I'd known he was for sale," I sighed. "We might have made an offer. Guess it's too late now."

"Yes, I believe they have him consigned at the sale," Mike relayed. "I'll let you know if anything changes."

"Please do so."

On Monday following the sale, I stopped at the stable to check on Stormy. To my amazement, the palomino was back in the pen with our boy. Apparently, due to Spud's age, the highest bid was twelve hundred dollars, so the owners "no-saled" Spud and hauled him back home. I wasted no time in getting the owner's contact information and finding out more details. I found out that he was originally going to be purchased by the Waterloo Police Department for their Equine Unit, but Spud was one-half inch short of the height requirement set by the department. The owners brought him to Mike's stable to hopefully find a buyer. At the time, Mike didn't know I was interested in Spud, nor did I know that Spud was for sale. In the end, it worked out perfectly as the owners were anxious to sell. We acquired the attractive horse for one thousand dollars.

Spud didn't seem like an appropriate name for such a sweet, handsome horse. Since he *was* a palomino and Stormy's new best friend, I renamed him *Pal*. The golden horse seemed pleased with his new name, pricking his ears forward each him his name was called.

The Lone Survivor was no longer alone. He would live out the rest of his days beside his new forever friend, Pal.

Chapter 14
Storm Chaser

Over the next several years, Stormy and Pal became great pasture buddies, lounging in the shade of the tall white pines surrounding their main lot in the summer time, and sharing the warm, cozy lower section of the dairy barn in the winter months. Occasionally, Gary and I saddled the two horses up for a quick ride around the hay field as a relaxing way to end the day.

Subtle physical changes began to occur with Stormy during this time. He didn't shed out as quickly in the springtime; he developed fatty deposits over his shoulders and on his rump, and he had episodes of tenderness in his feet. I knew the symptoms all too well and was determined to keep Stormy as healthy as possible using holistic therapies, such as essential oils, homeopathic remedies, nutritional supplements, and quantum physics energy devices. My veterinary practice had changed to include holistic therapies after I was challenged by several major health issues, including breast cancer. Since the fear I had of chemo and radiation was so great, I turned to alternative medicine to get my body back in balance instead. Thrilled with my response to natural treatments, I expanded my education so I could use these noninvasive and gentle therapies in animals.

In June of 2014, I was invited to speak at Young Living Essential Oils International Grand Convention in Salt Lake City, Utah. My workshops were scheduled on June 24th and 25th. With travel time, I would be gone a total of five days. I was always apprehensive about leaving the animals for any length of time, but Gary assured me he would carefully watch over everyone in my absence. He promised to check the horses over morning and night, and to look at the electric fences and water tanks to make sure everything was operating correctly.

On the morning of my departure, I walked down to the lower barnyard to wish Pal and Stormy good-bye. The morning air was warm and thick with humidity. Severe storms were predicted for later in the day and for most of the week ahead. "Hey boys, please stay safe from the storms," I pleaded. "I'm going to be gone for a few days, but I'll be back soon. Love you both." I patted Stormy's neck and noticed his nostrils were flaring a bit and his chest was slightly damp with sweat. "Why don't you guys go hangout in the corncrib in front of the fan?" I suggested. "It's going to be a pretty warm day."

Gosh, I hope these storms hold off, I thought. I *know the horses are smart and they'll go wherever their instincts tell them, but I don't want to worry. Please look after them, God,* I prayed silently. *Keep them safe from harm.* I tried to shake off the uneasy feeling that nagged at me as I headed back toward the house.

Sometime between 9:00 p.m. on Tuesday, June 24th and 6:00 a.m. Wednesday, June 25th, Stormy Bey passed away from what appeared to be a massive heart attack or aneurysm. Gary discovered his lifeless body at the bottom corner of the pasture before leaving for work on Wednesday. Stormy had absolutely no marks or signs of struggle. The only clue that he had a sudden and immediate death was that he bit his tongue hard, as if his heart had stopped before his body fell to the ground. Gary had just been petting him the evening before when Stormy came to the water tank for a drink. He had been perfectly fine then.

Words were not possible to describe the devastating feelings we felt over the passing of "Beautiful Boy." We both felt incredible guilt over the situation, although subconsciously both knew there was nothing that could have stopped his death. Many tears were shed as Gary described in detail the events of Stormy's death, his burial, and trying to figure out how to tell me that my beautiful friend had passed away.

I knew deep in my heart that this was Stormy's "plan." Ever since I threw my arms around his neck and said, "Don't you die on me too!" after Ty and Ibn's passings, I felt Stormy *chose* to end his twenty-two year old life on earth when I wasn't around to witness it. The odd feeling I had on the morning I said goodbye to Pal and Stormy was confirmation that Stormy had a plan in mind. The fact that he chose to die in a corner of the pasture closest to Ty and Ibn's graves were another indication of Stormy's intentions.

I always felt that Stormy wished to be with the other two horses, making the trio united again. Even though he loved Pal, the pull to be with his friends in spirit was too great for him to remain in the present realm.

A few months following Stormy's death, I received a call from a woman who was desperately looking for a home for her Arabian gelding. She was boarding three horses and the monthly boarding bill was too much for her budget. The gelding had sustained a suspensory ligament injury in one of his rear legs, and had been stalled for over a year with five minutes of hand-walking daily. His injury was supposedly not getting better. Her veterinarian had recommended euthanasia because he convinced the owner it would never heal.

When I heard this, I immediately became interested in looking at the gelding. Although Pal had a pasture buddy, it was another horse that my friends had "loaned" me until they found a permanent mate. I instructed the woman to *not even consider* euthanasia. At least not until I could look at him. For whatever reason, I had a good gut feeling about this horse.

The instant I saw the beautiful bay Arabian gelding, I fell in love. "Airs" had huge, lovely brown eyes and a sweet, friendly personality. He sniffed me all over with his soft muzzle as I scratched him gently under his mane. When Airs' owner walked him around the indoor arena, there was no evidence of lameness. I didn't even care if Airs was rideable or not; I just wanted to find a forever friend for Pal. However, I was confident that with my arsenal of natural therapies, Airs could return to full function.

Airs' owner provided me with his registration papers. I didn't really care about them except I *was* curious to find out his lineage. I had a sneaking suspicion that there was some connection to Stormy in the genealogy. I was shocked, though, when the entire sire's line was *exactly* the same as Stormy's. No wonder I was drawn to this sweet and attractive horse!

Airs' contract of sale was for a mere dollar, to make it a "formal" sale. Airs' owner was just relieved to find him a good home and to be out from under the cumbersome boarding bill. We were thrilled to have another great horse in the family and a partner for Pal.

Gary and I thought about changing his name but had difficulty finding just the right one. Our friend and natural horsemanship trainer, Bob, came up with a clever idea. "Hey, you two are storm spotters. You like to chase storms. Stormy is this guys' predecessor, so how about "Storm Chaser?" You can call him Chaser or Chase for short."

"Perfect, Bob!" I smiled. "Thanks for the input. Chase it will be."

Some Photographs

Gentle Ty with seven-year old Carrie

Gary's daughter, Sierra, posing for senior pictures with Stormy

Carrie and Ibn in the warmup arena before their first Rodeo Queen contest

Carrie and Ty getting ready for an
English Pleasure Walk-Trot class

Barbara and Ty getting ready for
a dressage clinic

Ty and Barbara winning the State Country Pleasure Championship in Des Moines, Iowa

Carrie preparing Stormy for an
English Pleasure class

Carrie and Ibn performing the Queen Salute at
their 2nd Rodeo Queen contest

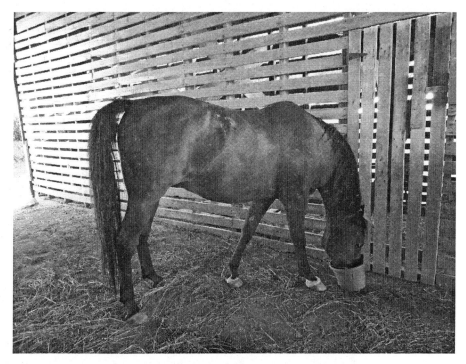

Stormy eating his supplements for Cushing's syndrome
 —note the excessive fat deposits on his shoulders, hips and rump.

Ibn showing off his favorite trick
 —sticking out his tongue

Barbara astride Ibn right before he was officially retired from riding

Acknowledgments

I am blessed to have had such great support for the writing of this book. It took courage and working through tears to get the words into print.

First of all, thanks from the bottom of my heart to my husband and best friend, Gary, who encouraged and motivated me to take on this project.

To Jim Mayhew, my brother and also my coach—I can't express enough gratitude for your belief in me and your ability to motivate me to finish the book.

To Laura Ashton, my author assistant, who has provided me with keen insights and has been there for me, thank you.

To Patrick Naville, thank you for your amazing inspiration and encouragement. Your mentoring has been a godsend.

To all my family and friends who are animal lovers and are advocates for their wellbeing, thank you.

Dr Barbara Fox

About the Author

Barbara Fox, DVM. has been a practicing veterinarian for the past twenty-three years. She is owner of Beyond Tradition Animal Healing Center, a holistic veterinary practice, and has spoken across the United States about the benefits of natural therapies. She and her husband, Gary, live near Wadena, Iowa, with their two horses, Pal and Chaser, and their eight house cats. In her spare time, Barbara loves hiking, reading, and spending time in the San Juan mountains of Colorado.